Cambridge Wizard Student Guide

The Truman Show
directed by Peter Weir
Elective *Image*

Richard McRoberts B.A., M.Ed., M.A.C.E.

Marcia Pope B.A., M.A., Grad. Dip. Children's Lit.

CAMBRIDGE
UNIVERSITY PRESS

PUBLISHED BY THE PRESS SYNDICATE OF THE UNIVERSITY OF CAMBRIDGE
The Pitt Building, Trumpington Street, Cambridge, United Kingdom

CAMBRIDGE UNIVERSITY PRESS
The Edinburgh Building, Cambridge CB2 2RU, UK
40 West 20th Street, New York, NY 10011–4211, USA
477 Williamstown Road, Port Melbourne 3207, Australia
Ruiz de Alarcón 13, 28014 Madrid, Spain
Dock House, The Waterfront, Cape Town 8001, South Africa

http://www.cambridge.edu.au

First published in 2004

Cover design by Cressaid Media
Cover art Valerie den Ouden
Typeset by Kath Puxty

Printed in Australia by Print Impressions

Typeface Berkeley System PageMaker® [KP]

National Library of Australia Cataloguing in Publication data
    McRoberts, Richard, 1948- .
    The Truman Show, directed by Peter Weir : elective, image.

    For HSC standard English students.
    ISBN 0 521 54615 X

    1. The Truman show (Motion picture). 2. Motion
    picures – Study and teaching (Secondary). 3.
    Reality television programs – Study and teaching
    (Secondary). I. Pope, Marcia. II. Title. III. Title :
    Elective, image : The Truman show, directed by
    Peter Weir. (Series : Cambridge wizard students guide).
791.4372

ISBN 0 521 54615 X

Contents

Elective 3: *Image*

General outline of the elective

The HSC Standard course includes, under Module A (Experience through Language), Elective 3: *Image*.

This invites students to 'explore the nature of images and the ways they are used in everyday situations'. As well as the prescribed text (in this case Peter Weir's film *The Truman Show*), study involves considering other examples of 'visual representations' in everyday life, and the need to 'explore the relationships and attitudes established in the communication of images' as well as 'textual features' of the 'medium' and 'mode' of communication. The elective descriptor ends by inviting students to consider how images 'shape meaning' and how aspects of the world are 'represented' through images.

Introduction: The Notion of Image

Our 'image-rich' environment

Images dominate our world. It is estimated that we see an astonishing 36,000 advertising images in a week – and that's not counting all the other images we 'consume' by way of the media – nor all the things we see in the course of our everyday lives which are not 'constructed'. We live in an image-rich environment, and not surprisingly, this has some effect on how we think (including our sense of values) and the way we act. The following notes offer some basic ideas about visual communication, and the importance of 'image' and 'representation'.

The importance of visual communication

The dominance of visual senses

Scientists have established beyond any doubt that our visual senses are dominant. What we *see* has far more impact on us than what we hear (let alone touch, taste, or smell).

Case study

Consider a simple example. You are 18 years old, and have just saved up for your first car. It has been offered very cheap for private sale. The ad read 'A1 condition. A real goer. An absolute bargain.' You are looking it over, while the owner stands by. It is shiny and fast looking. However, you notice some oil on the concrete under the engine. 'What's that?' you ask. 'Oh that,' he replies, 'that's from my previous car. Don't worry about it.' You start the car up. A cloud of blue smoke comes out the exhaust. 'Is it burning oil?' you ask. 'Nah. It's just cold,' he says. 'And those kilometres…they're genuine?' you ask, because they're almost too good to believe. 'Too right,' he says in honeyed tones, adding, 'Would I lie to you?' Then you notice that he is perspiring a little, although it's not a hot day. You stand there, scratching your head. Are you going to buy this car?

Clearly, in this example, what you *see* (the oil, the smoke and the body language of the seller) are going to override both his words and the rhapsodic text of the ad. Your eyes are telling you something quite different to what you read and what you heard (from him). If you have any sense, you are not likely to go ahead.

Research has demonstrated that in a face-to-face situation, the breakdown of meaning (or what you really take notice of) is like this:

Quote

Body language	70%
Verbal information (tone, etc)	23%
Words (ie what is said)	9%

Images beat words by seven to one

Let's translate: what you *see* is infinitely more significant (seven times more meaningful) than the words you hear. The old adage that we can only trust it if we see it with our own eyes is true.

This information has been exploited quite deliberately by modern day media practitioners. Consider the way products are 'represented' in TV ads, or the way film stars are shot in feature films. Products (whether they be things or people) are presented in an *ideal* way. The butter always looks yummy and melts beautifully on the muffin. The actress always looks gorgeous, no matter where she is. The 'real world' (the butter when it goes rancid, the actress on a bad hair day) is kept out of the shot.

Types of visual representations

Since time immemorial, humankind has made images. We seek to 'represent' (reproduce, replicate) the real world in a visual form. Cave paintings dating back some 40,000 years have been discovered in central and northern Australia, and similar ones are to be found in Europe. The very earliest types of writing – Egyptian hieroglyphics, Sumerian cuniform (which eventually developed into the 'Greek' alphabet) and Chinese ideograms – were all *originally* picture writing. A picture of the sun was used, for instance, to represent the idea of the sun. Although all writing systems later morphed into purely symbolic form – the prototypes were invariably pictorial (ie image based).

Ancient examples of image making

Our species has always been obsessed with representing the world pictorially. Not only are we fascinated by anything visual, but we love to try and value things and achieve permanence by fixing objects in a visual form. There is a long but strong connection between the simple stick figures of small children and the greatest works of masters such as Rembrandt or Renoir. Both are doing the same thing – representing 'reality' in images – only the level of skill differs.

Image-making a universal concern

A consequence of this obsession with image-making has been the long history of permanent representations or 'art'. What do we represent?

Consistent themes in image making

• **Deities** (gods) in visual forms – both anamorphic (ie in human shape, such as Greek statues) and non-figurative (ie not showing the 'shape' of the god, but representing it symbolically, as in the monumental and 'perfect' form of ancient temples). This tradition has continued throughout human history, as a study of any church, mosque (although figurative representations of God are forbidden in Muslim tradition) or temple will show.

• **Significant individuals** (such as kings, emperors, great generals, wealthy men and women) in visual forms eg paintings, statues, tapestries (like William the Conqueror in the Bayeux Tapestry), coins, heraldic emblems and the like. These are almost always presented in an idealised form. Court painters or sculptors knew that they trod a fine line between matching the 'likeness' of their subject, but also making him/her look as good as possible. (This tradition continues in the modern world with the way politicians' 'minders' package the image of their masters to make them as attractive as possible to voters.)

• **Idealised forms** of men and women – the 'perfect' woman (eg Mona Lisa, by Leonardo) or the 'perfect' man (eg David, by Michelangelo). Although such notions are 'subjective', there are in fact widely agreed attitudes – in a given culture – about what constitutes beauty in both men and women. This tradition continues in the modern world – as a glance at any fashion or film magazine will confirm. Although notions of beauty change with time – consider how the Marilyn Monroe paradigm (1950s template) has given way to the Kylie Minogue paradigm (current template) – at any given moment there will a broad agreement about what 'sexy' or 'gorgeous' looks like. This in turn has huge cultural impact, as ordinary men and women adjust how they look to match images of the 'ideal' presented to them in the media.

• **Institutions, goods and services** – which will involve some combination of imagery (a logo, like that of the Commonwealth Government, a public 'face', like that of the AAMI girl, a piece of animated vision, like the Dreamworks corporate 'vision') and text. In the old days, institutions or business houses had to content themselves with noble insignia. Nowadays, all the trickery of the electronic media are at their disposal.

Means of visual representations

Indeed, the 'modern' age has seen a veritable explosion in means for visually representing the world. Here are some key technological breakthroughs and their dates:

Significant dates in the development of visual media

• 1455 – invention of **printing** by movable type by Johannes Gutenberg (beginning of the 'modern age' of print publishing)
• 1822 – invention of **photography** by Niepce
• 1887 – invention of celluloid **film** by Goodwin (basis of all modern photography and the movie industry)
• 1888 – invention of the **'Kodak' camera** by George Eastman (basis of 'home use' photography)
• 1893 – invention of the cinematograph (**movie camera**) by the Lumière brothers (basis of the movie industry)
• 1926 – demonstration by John Logie Baird of **'television'** (though his version was later supplanted by American technology): TV dates in Australia from 1956 (black and white) and 1975 (colour)
• 1928 – Walt Disney introduces Mickey Mouse and the whole genre of **animated feature films** to the world (as well as founding a media empire of huge cultural importance)
• 1946 – construction of the first electronic digital **computer** (basis of the internet and all digital vision products)
• 1970s - 1980s – invention of the **internet**
• 1991 – invention of the **World Wide Web**.

On the basis of these technologies, we now have the power to create and transmit images around the world in seconds. Ask your grandparents what media 'images' they had access to as children and you will see how far we have come.

The mass media

Defining the mass media

The term '**mass media**' is vital to this discussion. The word 'media' is simply the *plural* of 'medium' (a means of transmitting or communicating), and 'mass' signifies large numbers of people simultaneously. A mainstream movie will be viewed by millions of people. A satellite broadcast of Olympic Games will be seen by billions around the world.

Let's remind ourselves what the 'mass media' are:

Types of mass media

• **Newspapers**: a medium combining visual representations (photos, cartoons, advertising images and diagrams) and text – with the emphasis more on text in 'serious' newspapers and more on images in 'popular' newspapers.
• **Magazines**: a medium combining visual representations (photos, advertising images) and text – with the emphasis more on images.
• **Radio** (not a visual medium).
• **Television**: a medium combining image (both still and moving), sound and text – with the images normally considered dominant.
• **Movies** (or **cinema**): a medium combining images (live action or animated or CGI) and sound – with the images dominant.
• **The Internet**: a medium combining images and text – with the balance varying enormously according the website involved (almost all have images of some kind).

Influence of the mass media

As these media have developed, and become part of every-day life, their influence on us has increased proportionately. The more *visually-oriented* media tend to have the greatest influence. Research has shown that when asked 'What do you believe?', people will nominate television as the medium they most trust, following by newspapers, magazines and radio. The reason for this goes back to what we said about the dominance of visual communication. We tend to believe what we see. That we tend to believe this too easily, and remain largely unaware of the 'constructed' nature of visual information, is an important part of the debate (see below).

Codes, genres and conventions of visual communication

The different 'media' work in different ways. We can break this down into three key concepts:

Terms used
in discussion
of mass
media

(1) **Codes** – signs or 'signifiers' within a media product (like a movie) that have an understood meaning (eg for an action film, the handsome, muscly guy is the hero, in a sci fi movie the villain is ugly and dresses in black, etc). The idea of a 'code' therefore refers largely to a sign or event with an established meaning.

(2) **Genres** – another word for 'form' or type. This refers to the different varieties of product within a medium, eg romance, comedy, thriller, horror, biopic, musical, etc.

(3) **Conventions** – the usual patterns or internal forms of a particular genre. Just as a business letter has standard 'conventions' (Dear Sir or Madam, formal language, Yours sincerely, etc) so media forms have standard patterns. We expect an 'action' movie to have assorted chase sequences, gunfights, explosions, daring adventures involving hi-tech gagetry, and so on. We expect a romance to have a good looking man and a woman, who meet and fall in love, but for some reason can't finally get together until the end of the movie. These conventions are not as strong as 'rules', but are strong enough to set the expectations of most viewers as they engage with a media text.

There is no room here to exhaustively survey the codes, genres and conventions of all the visual media, but it might help to ask yourself these questions. An example is given below to suggest how to go about this analysis.

Think of a particular medium (eg television) and ask:

Questions to
ask of a
mass
medium

• What are the usual genres that we have come to expect of this medium (eg types of TV program)?
• What are well known examples of each genre?
• Choose a particular genre. What are the usual conventions of this genre (eg visual design, dress codes, characters, etc)?
• What sorts of elements (storyline, characters, dress, location,

etc) would be considered inappropriate for this genre?

• Can you identiy examples of manipulation (possibly distortion or falsification) that would have gone on 'behind the scenes' (eg CGI, voice dubbing, etc)? What are examples of this?

How the visual media shape meaning

The illusion that the media show us 'reality'

It is a common misconception that the visual representations we see in the media are 'natural' or 'real'. We hear that 'The camera never lies'. This belief assumes that what we see is 'all there is', or, put another way, that the people behind the media representation simply put up pictures of 'reality', without interfering or interpreting in any way.

Representations are constructed

This is *not* the case. All media products are 'constructed'. This means that they are deliberately put together in certain ways so as to satisfy certain purposes, whether explicit or just 'understood'.

Case study: tabloid current affairs TV

Let's take a 'tabloid' (or popular mass audience) television current affairs show. The unspoken assumptions that inform the work of all behind the scenes personnel include such as these:

• **Drama** and 'human interest' is a vital ingredient in making the show 'good viewing' (ie exciting and talk-worthy). So a story about a 'battler' fighting a huge corporation, or two neighbours coming to blows over a fence or a pet, is more interesting than an important scientific discovery.

• **Popular** and 'man/woman in the street' is best. A story on diets is better than a story on discoveries in astronomy. A story on pop stars and their drug problems is better than a story on the environment.

• **Images** of the subject are vital – no pictures, no story. Pictures are *so* important that they may need to be faked. This is why 'reconstructions' or 'dramatisations' are so common, why 'archive footage' is so often used (any war, any cyclone, any picture of the city or person concerned) and why an interview with a silhouette is better than just the text of the interview alone.

• An 'angle' or **point of view** is essential – there is no 'mileage' in being 'wishy washy' and even-handed – it is better to mount a case of some kind. An example might be a story about a brutal government department crushing an innocent pensioner (thereby 'proving' that bureaucrats are unfeeling monsters).

• Keep things **simple**. Black and white (or absolute right and absolute wrong) is preferred. Shades of grey (maybe both sides have some validity) are confusing. Villains and heroes are indispensable. So hungry are certain tabloid programs for villains that they will actually go out and look for 'shonky' builders or rip off merchants, or chase up the drug problem – blowing both out of all proportion – in their attempt to make an exciting story.

It follows that if the media work to an 'agenda' (such as that outlined above for tabloid current affairs TV), they will shape the images (as well as sound and other aspects of the product) accordingly.

Case study: media manipulation in practice

Let's take an example. A current affairs show has decided to do a story on a property developer who is trying to put a holiday resort on a strip of prime coastline. Early in their editorial meetings, they decide on the 'angle': the developer is a greedy 'fat cat' who is just trying to make bucks, and will do anything to get his resort approved. The local protesters are honorable citizens who just want to keep their beach unspoiled. The reporter and camera crew go out on assignment *with the editorial angle already established*. They collect 'footage' to suit the pre-set agenda. Despite all their attempts to simplify the story, they still end up with the developer looking like a decent man, with plausible arguments. They still end up with the protesters looking like woolly radicals. So they 'doctor' the material a little. They choose a nice looking girl as representative of the protesters. They show her walking along the beach and run the voiceover of another (not very photogenic) protester over the top. They 'cut' all the plausible arguments offered by the developer, and leave only his statement that 'I'm not going to be pushed around by a bunch of hippies'. They omit the shots of the developer walking in shorts and thongs along the beach, and talking about how sympathetic he is to the environment, showing him only in his plush office. They shoot him from below to make him look powerful and menacing. They do 'cutaways' to the reporter (filmed separately) looking deeply disturbed by his answers. They shoot the protesters from above,

How meaning is shaped

to make them look powerless. They completely omit the chanting and slogan waving. End result: not one of the images in this story is fake, but the whole story has been set up to a preconceived agenda, which it 'argues' (unbeknown to the viewers) with devasting effectiveness.

What images communicate

Given that images are so powerful, whatever they 'argue' can have significant social consequences. The reason most commentators and politicians get so concerned about 'media bias' is because they know that the media are opinion shapers.

How images carry values

An image or 'representation' can be made to say anything at all, and indeed can be interpreted in any of a range of ways (for the *viewer* is part of the transaction, and brings his/her own ideology and and prejudices to the viewing). An image can carry a negative view, a positive view, or an evenhanded view. It can even be 'neutral', though media theorists suggest that **every** mediated product or **image** is '**value-laden**'. We may think we're just looking at a female newsreader, reading the news, but a feminist analyst will notice that the newsreader conforms to the 'blond dolly bird' stereotype of good looks, and therefore confirms the traditional sexist expectations on women about appearance. We may think we're just looking at a mindless action movie, but cultural analysts will see in its depiction of the villains as nasty orientals a racial argument that reinforces popular prejudices.

In analysing the meanings attached to constructed images, we should be aware of attitudes created towards such things as:

Key values/ issues to consider in analysing the media

• **Gender** – How are men depicted? How are women depicted? Is there any suggestion that there is a 'normal' or 'ideal' way of behaving for either sex? How are gays depicted? Are stereotypes involved in any way?

• **Race and culture** – How are people from other races and cultures depicted? As superior? As inferior? As 'funny' or primitive? Is the focus on their 'humanity', and their needs, or on their dress, their accents, their cultural or religious objects? Are stereotypes involved in any way?

• **Politics** – How are the political adversaries (or players) depicted? Is one side favoured over the other (by such means as those discussed above regarding the current affairs show – not by direct editorial comment usually)? Are minority groups given their say, or shown as comical or irrelevant? Are multiple points of view aired, or is there only one argument?

• **Public issues** eg drugs – How is the issue summarised? Is one 'right way of thinking' offered, or is a diversity allowed? Are certain viewpoints 'privileged' (favoured) while others are mocked? Is the issue simplified (eg there is one cause of drug addiction), or enriched? Are there villains and heroes? Are stereotypes involved in any way?

How 'true' are images of reality?

The above discussion signposts many of the key elements in this debate. It will be obvious from the examples that serious questions need to be asked about 'truth' and 'reality', as well as 'image'.

The problem of subjectivity Even in everyday life, these are slippery concepts. What is 'real'? What is 'right' or 'wrong'? Whose view (if anyone's) is the valid one? We know that we see the world from a 'subjective' (or personal) point of view. If someone criticises our essay, we are more inclined to protect our ego than to listen to the criticisms. If anyone attacks 'Australians', we are inclined to go into defensive mode, regardless of the charges. If someone praises us, we are more inclined to believe the praise than to ask, Why are they being so nice?

In talking of mediated images, or the media, the debate becomes even more vexed. Here we are talking not only of problematic notions like 'reality' and 'values', but are looking at an industry which is not – like us in private life – just reacting to events, but is in the business of actively constructing meanings.

Case study: women's magazine and image shaping Let's consider an example. A gossip magazine editor is looking through the latest celebrity photos. She finds, and chooses, a particularly nasty papparazzi shot of a well known actress (with no makeup and her stomach bulging). She already has a file photo of the same actress looking impossibly glamorous, but this picture is no use to her. She needs a 'story'. She instructs a staff writer to come up with 1000 words about how this actress is fighting a desperate and losing battle against weight gain. The writer can 'make it up', if she likes, unless she can find snippets of gossip to support the theory. The headline will be: 'Glamour puss to blob: XX's losing battle against the bulge'.

Now perhaps the inside story about 'gutter journalism' like this has leaked out. Perhaps people suspect everything they read, or see. But for every sophisticated media watcher who would see this story as a 'beat up', there are probably dozens of ordinary readers who simply believe every word. For the camera (image) never lies. Or does it? Can you think of your own (real) examples of the way the media twist reality to suit their purposes?

What do we bring to a 'reading' of images?

People's attitudes towards images vary enormously, of course. Our attitudes are informed by a range of principles, including the following:

The determinants of how we 'read' the meaning of images

• **Personal ideology** eg. a feminist will be very sensitive to any image which depicts women (or a woman) in a way which could be construed as sexist or 'patriarchal', or which appears to endorse traditional roles or to denigrate 'liberated' attitudes or roles (so she will 'read' *Pretty Woman* as a patriarchal text, because it shows the Julia Roberts character as being valued for her appearance and being subservient to the man)

• **Political orientation** eg a Labor voter will look at the current Prime Minister and see his personal faults 'written' in his face, whereas a Liberal will just see the man; a conservative will look at student demonstrators and see them as 'long-haired layabouts', whereas a radical will look at the same people and see them as freedom fighters and heroes

• **Gender, and sexual orientation** eg a gay pride activist will be pleased by 'queer' icons (and a film such as *Priscilla Queen of the Desert*), whereas a 'Moral Majority' hardliner will be appalled

• **Cultural 'agenda'** eg some people will see AFL and Rugby League imagery as patriotic, heroic and fascinating – while images of ballet or symphonic concerts would be seen as 'la-de-dah' or even 'poofy'; it goes without saying that ballet enthusiasts will take the reverse view, and probably see images of footballers as primitive or grotesque.

The issue of 'real' versus fictional

Another variable is whether or not the image is seen as 'real' or 'fictitional'. We have built in 'filters' when it comes to mediated images. For example, as has been observed by a number of commentators, many people 'enjoy' or at least tolerate images of violence when they know them to be fictitious – as in a Tarantino film (eg *Pulp Fiction*, *Kill Bill*) – but abhor them when they see them as real – as in a news broadcast or current affairs show.

There are several famously 'hot' topics of debate – most

notably violence and sex. A great many people object to both on television, and get very unhappy about gore in movies. Others argue that images of sex and violence are 'cathartic', and that seeing them in a fictitional form (where we know that these are just actors pretending to have sex or die) allows us to deal safely and at arm's length with the underlying issues. It all goes back to our existing 'belief systems'.

The politics of visual communication

Cultural and media theorists make no bones about it. The media, whether knowingly or not, are part of the 'politics' of a community. That is, they are part of the process by which opinions are shaped, reinforced or challenged.

The most obvious agents here are clearly the news media (including current affairs and magazine products). It is no surprise really that the ABC is forever being accused (by the Conservatives) of left-wing bias. Any 'construction' put upon political events must be selective, and any time it does not match the prevailing conservative agendas, it will (naturally) be seen as distorted.

How the media carry cultural/ political messages

But the media in general are carriers of cultural messages. Game shows can be said to 'argue' (suggest, endorse) a consumerist mentality, which sees winning money and prizes as the ultimate delight. Fashion magazines can be said to underwrite the oppression of women by patriarchal attitudes – the idea of women as 'sex objects' to be viewed and consumed by men. American sitcoms can be said to underpin the prevailing conservatism of US society, because they so rarely feature minority groups (blacks, gays, Hispanics, etc) and reinforce the dominant (ie white, 'straight') culture. Where minority groups are represented, they may be done so negatively (eg the villains are blacks).

In preparing your general thinking about 'Image', it might help to ask questions like these – about a particular media product or image:

Political questions to ask of media products

• What does this 'representation' (image) appear to argue?
• Is there an underlying ideology or cultural assumption? What assumptions are made about the audience or purpose of the product/image?
• Who would be offended by this product/image? Why?
• Who/what is marginalised or disadvantaged by this product/image?

• What stereotypes are involved in this product/image?
• What version of this product/image is *not* shown? What is the effect of this?
• Does this product/image offer a criticism of the dominant culture, or does it endorse it? Is is part of a broad pattern of criticism or one of endorsement?

How 'image' shapes people

One of the clearest examples of how mediated images exert a social effect is the matter of '**body image**'. Try this exercise. Type these words into an internet search engine. You will get literally thousands of sites. If you add in 'anorexia' and 'bulimia', the total runs to millions.

Why people are obsessed with image

Why? Because people are obsessed with how they look. Why are they obsessed? Certainly a good part of it is 'natural'. However, it is often argued that the modern media have encouraged a greater obsession by the way they confront people – women especially – with images of so-called *ideal* faces and bodies. Think of the number of women's magazines which offer advice on 'the perfect you', or makeovers, or the 'right' clothes, makeup, hair and so on. If someone who is a little anxious about her appearance is constantly seeing beautiful, slim models with perfect skin and hair, is she going to feel better about herself, or worse? As the *Savage Garden* classic 'Affirmation' says in one line, 'I believe that beauty magazines promote low self-esteem'. If we consider that some 60% of Australian women are on a diet at any one time, we have to assume that there is some kind of 'body image' problem.

The example of body image obsession

'Body dysmorphia' (loathing of one's body) has now been added to the list of psychological maladies which afflict many (especially women). Think of the famous (ie celebrity) cases of bulimia (Princess Diana), erratic dieting (Oprah Winfrey), anorexia (Karen Carpenter) and the extent to which popular magazines track the weight 'problems' of female film stars, and you have plentiful examples of this issue.

A slightly less pernicious, but equally pervasive, example, is the way the media shape people's idea of what they should wear (think of *Vogue* magazine), the way they should decorate their homes (think of *Country Style* or *House and Garden*), what car they should drive, and so on. We of course have the option of resisting such image shaping forces, but there can be little doubt that they are *trying* to mould us.

Are we defenceless victims of the media?

Let us put it as bluntly as this to make an important point. It *is* possible to exaggerate too much. The media can be, and often are, portrayed as devious purveyors of 'representations', which vary from mere manipulation to outright lying. As a *generalisation*, this is going too far, though there are examples enough to support such claims in some areas of the media.

People collaborate with the media

In fact, people *choose* much more than such a model allows. They are much more active. They *want* to view images. They consume images, and love celebrities, not because the media force them to but because it comes naturally. Spectatorship is built into human nature. Even the nastier aspects of our urge to look – such as a taste for voyeurism (looking secretly at other people in ways they would not welcome) – is a part of our nature. Think of what happens in a schoolyard when someone yells 'Fight!' We love to see filmstars or royalty at work and play because it feeds some fantasy to be like them. We watch movies which offer a fictitious viewing of other people's lives because we enjoy such vicarious experiences.

The need for a balanced view

In coming to *The Truman Show*, we must keep in mind that while the author and director *do* critique the media, they also show *us*, the spectators, as being part of the equation. The media are not just villains, and we (the audience) are not just victims. Life is more complicated than that.

The Prescribed Text:
The Truman Show

Notes on the Director

Peter Weir was born on 21 August 1944 in Sydney. His father was a successful real estate agent, and the youthful Peter had a comfortable childhood, living in Vaucluse. He attended Vaucluse High School and then went on to Scots College.

In 1962, he enrolled at the University of Sydney, studying arts and law. However, he found the course work dull and 'industrialised', so he dropped out after less than a year, and began working for his father. Selling houses was not really to his taste though. His artistic sensibilities were already well in evidence, as the nineteen year old Weir refused to sell places he did not like.

Formative experiences
So, in 1965, on the strength of the money he had made, he set off overseas, travelling by ship to Europe. A strange and formative experience took place on board the long ship cruise. There was no entertainment on the boat, so Weir and friends he had made decided to produce shows, which they made using the closed circuit TV system on board. They were inspired by the then cult-hit show, *The Mavis Bramston Show*, an early Australian satiric comedy success. The making of the sketches on board the ship awakened Weir to his hunger for creative endeavour, and the power of the visual image. 'I felt a tremendous excitement about what I was doing,' he said later. 'Suddenly, this [filmmaking] was very natural to me.' He also met Wendy, later to become his wife.

On returning from Europe, he joined Channel Seven in Sydney as a stage hand. With friend Grahame Bond (later to become famous as the title character in *The Aunty Jack Show*), he went on to produce his first short film, *Count Vim's Last Exercise* (1967). This

Early films
was a 15 minute satire about bureaucracy. It created sufficient interest for Weir to go on to his second film, once again a satire, *The Life and Flight of the Rev. Buck Shotte* (1968), about an eccentric American preacher and his new religion. On the basis of these successful shorts, Weir moved into television, directing film segments for his old favourite, *The Mavis Bramston Show*.

In 1969, he joined the Australian Commonwealth Film Unit (the precursor to Film Australia), which before the establishment of the Australian Film and Television School (1973) was a prime training ground for Australian movie people. At last Weir had found his destiny. 'It was like a school,' he said of the ACFU. 'It was the university that I had looked for in 1963.' There, in a supportive and safe environment, he could hone his skills as a director.

In 1970, he directed *Michael*, part of a three part AFCU production, which won the Grand Prix prize of the Australian Film Institute. In 1971, he made *Homesdale*, which won the AFI's Second Grand Prix. The following year, Weir returned to Europe on a travel grant, writing scripts and learning his craft on feature film sets in England. On his return, he continued to direct short films for the ACFU.

First notable film

It was in 1974 that Weir directed his first feature film, *The Cars That Ate Paris*. The story concerns a small Australian town, Paris, besieged by a group of hoodlums in outlandishly customised cars (one has porcupine-like spines growing out of it). The film is bizarre but unforgettable. It was not a box office success, but it attracted considerable critical interest, enough to allow Weir to make his next film, and first great triumph.

The breakthrough: Picnic at Hanging Rock

Picnic at Hanging Rock (1975) was in every way a breakthrough film. Based on the Joan Lindsay novella of the same name, it concerns a party of schoolgirls who in 1900 vanished without trace from the famous natural monolith, Hanging Rock, not far from Woodend, to the north of Melbourne. The sheer beauty of the film, a lush period piece, let alone its beguiling storyline, assured its warm reception, both here and overseas. It was also the first serious Australian film to gain wide recognition in what has been called the renaissance of the local film industry. Here was a superbly professional movie, with great box office potential but also real artistic credentials, which triumphed at both local and international film festivals. It virtually became the symbol of the new Australian film industry. It also made Weir an international star.

His next feature had an American star, Richard Chamberlain, and international financial backing. *The Last Wave* (1977) concerns a lawyer (Chamberlain), who becomes involved in the defence of Aborigines and is recognised by them as a spiritual heir to their heritage.

Gallipoli

He followed it with another blockbuster success, *Gallipoli* (1981). Written by famous Australian playwright David Williamson, and starring the soon to be famous Mel Gibson, it concerns a pair of friends who are sports rivals in Western Australian before 'joining up' and being shipped to Gallipoli. The film, visually magnificent, emotionally charged and with a powerful anti-war sentiment underpinning it, was an enormous success. It gained nine AFI awards and made a lot of money.

In 1982, Weir followed up with *The Year of Living Dangerously*, based on the Christopher Koch novel of the same name. It concerns an Australian journalist, Guy Hamilton (Mel Gibson again) sent to cover the political turmoil in Indonesia during the Sukarno regime. Hamilton meets up with an English woman (played by Sigourney Weaver, newly famous because of *Alien*), and they have a torrid love affair against a background of danger and political intrigue. The film was beautiful to look at and highly exciting. Weir was by now a name director.

Move to America

His move to America followed. Weir accepted the offer of Paramount to direct a crime thriller set among the Amish of Pennsylvania. The film was called *Witness*, and starred Harrison Ford. It became one of the most acclaimed films of 1985, a box office hit that picked up no less than eight Oscar nominations, including those for Best Actor and Best Director.

The Mosquito Coast (1986), also with Harrison Ford, followed, though it was not a great box office success. It concerns an eccentric, Allie Fox (Ford) who abandons what he regards as the corrupt society of America to go and live among the simple people of the Mosquito Coast, in Central America. There he tries to set up a Utopia, with disastrous consequences.

Dead Poet's Society

In 1989, however, Weir had another hit, with *Dead Poet's Society*. Starring the charismatic Robin Williams in the part of inspiring teacher John Keating, a man who urges his students (in an uptight New England private school in 1959) to 'seize the day', and live life to the full. It proved a great success, again bridging the gap between 'art house' and popular viewing.

Green Card

Weir's next film, *Green Card* (1990) was even more successful. With French star Gerard Depardieu and American favourite Andie McDowell in the lead roles, it concerns a Frenchman arranging a bogus marriage with an American woman in order to obtain a 'green card' (work visa). Predictably, this fake relationship turns into a real one, with a powerful romantic climax. Although a mainstream romance, the movie is lovingly shot and features a striking soundtrack, as well as flawless performances by the leads. It has remained an all time favourite amongst moviegoers.

In 1993, Weir directed *Fearless*, based on the novel by Rafael Yglesias, about a group of people who survive a plane crash. Among them is one, played by Jeff Bridges, who believes he has become invulnerable. He becomes increasingly reckless with his life, until another near-death experience restores him to a sense of normality. Although featuring name stars and peppered with Weir's trademark lyrical images and seriousness, and a critical success, the film made little impression with the moviegoing public.

The Truman Show

In 1998, after a considerable interval, Weir again hit the headlines, with *The Truman Show*, a post-modern fantasy about a man, Truman Burbank (Jim Carrey) whose whole life is a 'reality TV' show. Truman discovers finally that his life is a fraud, and eventually escapes the show. The film is powerful and involving, and shows Carrey in one of his very few serious roles. It was another box office hit. The film is based on a script written in 1993 by Andrew Niccol (writer/director of the 1997 SF movie *Gattaca*). Niccol explained his interest in this subject as follows:

> Quote

I often felt people were lying to me...I used to think the idea was lucidrously farfetched, but [as the 90s media circus became more extreme] now I have to wonder....We decided to make [Truman] a prisoner in paradise.

The movie was released to widespread praise, and did well at the box office. Weir has since completed only one other film, *Master and Commander* (2003), a historical drama starring Russell Crowe.

Peter Weir is widely accepted as one of the few genuine Australian film 'auteurs' (directors with a personal vision and considerable creative control). Despite the many box office 'hits' he has had, and his long association with major studios, he is taken very seriously as a director whose work is always of high quality.

Reading a Film as Text

Studying a film requires skills similar to those used in working with a print text, such as analysis of narrative, characters, dialogue, theme and so on. It also requires consideration of other elements which are specific to cinema. Brief notes on these follow.

Actors and Acting

On the page, a text has only words to stimulate the reader's response. On film, performances bring the story to life in a critical way. Who plays a part, and how it is played, are crucial to the success of the work.

Jim Carrey

The choice of Jim Carrey for the central role of Truman was a crucial one. Carrey was of course best known for his many comic roles, such as *Ace Ventura* (1994) and *Dumb and Dumber* (1994). Although he is celebrated for his highly physical form of comedy and his elastic face, he also has the intelligence to played a straight part – and his charm was useful to the role.

The toothy grins in which Carrey specialises and his bodily energy well match the idea of the show (and Seahaven) as 'feelgood' reality TV. All – at least on the surface – is cheer and wholesomeness. But the quieter Carrey, glimpsed in scenes like the flashback to the 'drowning' (16), express a totally different idea – the emptiness behind the mask of all-American happiness. Above all, there is a sort of boyish innocence about Carrey, which perfectly suits the notion of a man naïve enough to be the unwitting subject of a TV show.

Supporting actors

Supporting actors are equally well cast. Laura Linney has played a variety of dramatic roles, including *Lorenzo's Oil* (1992) and *Primal Fear* (1996). The dominant impression however is her all-American blond good looks. Hers is the ideal face for an 'apple pie' American wife. Even her dimples work to underpin the (false) innocence of the role. Ed Harris too was a seasoned veteran, with strong parts in such movies as *The Right Stuff* (1983), where he played square-jawed pioneer astronaut John Glenn, *The Firm* (1993) and *Apollo 13*.

Mise en scene

This French expression is used by scholars to refer to the 'look' of the film, particularly the sets and locations in which the action takes place, the costumes and other objects on view, and the use of colour and lighting.

Sets, locations and the film's narrative 'space'

The Truman Show is unusual in that it is not only dominated by 'sets' – both internal and external – but that these are so stylised. Whereas many films use 'real' locations to give a feeling of 'authenticity', or at least backlot sets that mimic real cities or other spaces, *The Truman Show* does the reverse. It provides viewers with visual spaces that are all homogenised into a Disneyland-style prettiness.

Sets 'inside' the show

The major set, and dominant 'space' of the film, is 'Seahaven', a town of wide, tree-lined streets, cute houses, brand new office buildings and shops. Interiors are the same – homely, discreetly luxurious, with cheery colours and all the fittings – like what you find in a housing display village. Seahaven is a visual embodiment of the all-American dream of a perfect small town. This of course argues something. Here is, as Cristof puts it, 'the way the world should be'. Although it pretends to be 'reality', it is an idealised small town as imagined by Hollywood.

The only serious alternative to Seahaven is the Lunar Room (Cristof's space high above the Seahaven sound stage, behind the 'moon' that hangs in the Seahaven sky). This is designed in a minimalist, 'heaven'-like way – all bright light and airiness – to connote Cristof's god-like power over the show (and implicitly the control the media have over our lives in general).

Sets outside the show (alternative spaces)

There are a number of 'cutaway' scenes showing the show's audience in what purports to be the real world – the garage, the bar, the lounge room of the two old ladies, the bathroom of the fat man – but these are few and far between. A significant alternative space is Sylvia's apartment, which is full of lifelike clutter, its walls plastered with 'Save Truman' posters and suchlike. The visual styling of these 'real world' spaces is in strong contrast to the bland prettiness of Seahaven, subtly underscoring Cristof's point that the real world is disorderly and uncontrolled.

Camera angles and point of view

Placement of the camera is an important film technique. Most often the camera is placed at eye level with the actors to give the spectator a sense of participating in what is going on and being said.

However, shooting a character from above or below is also used to make subtle points. For instance, in Scene 9, we see Truman from high above – as the studio light crashes down onto the set beside him. This startling change of viewpoint is one of the early indications that Truman is a creature on a show, controlled from 'above'. Another such example is the crane shot used in Scene 41, where Truman drives his car around the roundabout. Again, his powerlessness – and indeed the absurdity of his situation (round and round meaninglessly) is visually reinforced.

High angle shots

Point of view is strongly underlined often in this movie, and reminds us that Truman is the object of people's continuous gaze. The very first scene in which we see him (2) shows his face *inside* a screen (which is itself onscreen). It is the bathroom mirror cam, and he is looking straight into it. This shocks us. We see instantly that he is looking into a camera lens – in other words it fore-grounds the idea of a *lens*, of *spectatorship*.

Camera frame shots

A number of shots are taken from highly unusual viewpoints. Think of the distorted 'fisheye' angle showing twins Don and Ron (11), obviously taken from the camera clearly visible at the top of the Kaiser Chicken advertising billboard, or the deskcam (12), showing Truman on the phone (but shot from *below* his desk). At intervals throughout the film, particularly once the 'secret' is out (and Truman knows his life is being filmed), we see how Cristof deliberately chooses a point of view. Think of the dashboard cam (10, 31 and others), the pencil sharpener cam (70) and the mast cam (88) – as especially unusual examples.

Shot types and framing

Long shots show a whole scene. They are typically establishing shots, as when we see Seahaven town square the first time (11), or when we see Truman and Lauren (Sylvia) on the beach (27). These enable us to locate the context for the action to be shown in medium shot or even close up. Extreme long shots are very rare.

Long shots

Medium shots (the most common) show part of a scene. They may be whole figure shots, as in the many scenes involving

Medium shots

Truman and Meryl or Truman and Marlon, or the shots inside cars. Medium shots are a half way point between long and close up shots, and are the most common in carrying on the story.

Close up shots

Close up shots are for significant detail, or for highly involving moments. In these, the camera moves right up to the characters, as if we could touch them. They are used to great effect in the library scene (26), in which Truman first meets Lauren, and the embrace scene (27), in which we as viewers are only centimetres away from the lovers. In watching their reactions, we are led to share in them, thereby enormously heightening our emotional involvement in the story.

Framing

Framing can mean what type of shot is used, but it can also refer to what the director puts *inside* the view he presents. Truman is often shot in images with framing devices, like doorways and windows. While these items are naturalistic features, and perhaps don't draw attention to themselves, they position him as 'confined' and controlled. Even more significant perhaps are those shots where the fact that a camera lens is involved is deliberately underlined. There is one long shot in Scene 11 where a camera follows Truman in telephoto mode, and in vignette (ie with an area of black in a circle around the central image). Scene 13 involves no less than four separate vignette angles (cams): the approach to the jetty; the view of Truman at the ticket window, taken from behind the ticket man's head in the booth – the latter 'panning' to follow Truman and revealing a glass prism effect around the image; the bollard cam (on the jetty next to the sunken boat; and the overhead cam shot as Truman stops at the sunken boat). Most of the early shots in Scene 37 (the hospital scene) involve deliberate prism or dark vignette surrounds (to remind us that Truman is being filmed). Most of the shots in Scene 38 (the travel agent) are taken from very strange angles, as if from hidden cameras built into the décor. These self-consciously stylised shots are reminders that Truman is the object of voyeuristic scrutiny. It is not normal for filmmakers to draw attention to their art. Characters do not look into the lens. Lenses are not 'signposted' – they are just used ('invisibly'). *The Truman Show* breaks these rules as a way of pointing out the act of viewing itself.

Lens and vignette frames

Editing

Joining two shots together makes a connection between them in our mind. It is also a key element in the way the director paces the narrative. At its most obvious, it links them in time (and usually space). For example, Scene 27 (the abduction of Sylvia) is followed immediately by Scene 28 (the bar cutaway scene) in which the waitress explains to her colleague how Truman wanted to follow Sylvia, but was prevented by his mother's fake illness.

Cross-cutting As the secret of Truman's fake life is revealed, and the connection between Cristof and the story is made explicit, we see some striking uses of editing. For instance, think of Marlon's 'I'd never lie to you' scene (46, 48), in which we are startled by hearing the same words uttered by Marlon and Cristof, as Cristof feeds the actor his lines.

Editing also has to do with a scene's tempo. Consider the 'storm at sea' scenes (91, 93), which are 'cut' very rapidly, to convey a sense of drama and peril. In contrast, the interview with Cristof (94) is long and leisurely, to suggest control and power.

Sound

Unlike literary texts, films have both a powerful visual and an auditory dimension. Let us not forget the way sound is used as a signifier of meaning, and a way of manipulating the viewer.

It goes without saying that dialogue is important in this film. Key psychological or thematic information is often located in exchanges between characters. What of the radio transmissions (31), or the marvellous duplication of lines between Marlon and Cristof (47-48), both making important (and startling) points about artificiality? Then there are the totally non-verbal sound elements – the sound effects (think of the 'rip' sound when Truman's boat punctures the sea cyclorama – the music (think of the romantic piano track over the red cardigan scene, or the synthetic 'weepie' music over the reunion). All these are part of cinematic 'language'.

Summary of the Film

1 The lunar room

Cristof is being interviewed. He looks straight at the camera, and says:

> We've become bored with watching actors give us phoney emotions – tired of pyrotechnics and special effects. While the world he inhabits is in some respects counterfeit, there's nothing fake about 'The Truman Show' – no scripts, no cue cards. It isn't always Shakespeare, but it is a life.

2 Truman's bathroom, day

Truman is play acting in the mirror, imagining himself the hero of a great adventure (this one about climbing to the top of a mountain, 'broken legs and all'). We see his face inside what is obviously the viewfinder of a TV camera.

3 The lunar room

Cristof adds that many viewers 'leave him on all night for comfort'.

4 Truman's bathroom, day

Truman continues his imaginative adventures.

5 On the Seahaven set, exterior, day

'Meryl' is being interviewed. She says:

> There is no difference between a private life and a public life. My life is my life – is 'The Truman Show'. 'The Truman Show' is a lifestyle. It's a noble life. It is ... a truly blessed life.

6   Truman's bathroom, day

Once more we see Truman acting out an imaginative part in the mirror (this time he will die and the other members of the expedition will use him 'as an alternative source of food').

7 Studio

'Marlon' is being interviewed. He says:

Quote

It's all true. It's all real. Nothing here is fake. Nothing you see on this show is fake. It's merely controlled.

8 Truman's bathroom, day

Truman is pretending (to order his men to eat him). We hear a voice call out, 'Truman, you're going to be late!'. He calls OK and reluctantly leaves the mirror and the bathroom.

9 Outside Truman's house, day

Truman comes out the front door, dressed for work. He is greeted by his neighbours, a cheery 'black' family. He calls out 'Good morning!' adding '**In case I don't see you, good afternoon, good evening and good night!**'

As he makes his way to the car, another neighbour (Spencer) comes by with a big dog (Pluto). The dog jumps on Truman, scaring him. He prepares to get into the car.

Just at that moment, a strange object falls from the sky. It crashes to the footpath nearby. Truman goes across to examine it. It is a smashed light of the kind used in TV studios. Truman is mystified.

10 Truman's car, day

Truman is driving to work. A news flash on the radio reports a plane in trouble over Seahaven – but no one was hurt. People talk on the radio. Truman joins in cheerfully.

11 Seahaven city square, day

Truman's car drives into the centre of town, which is bustling with life.

Moments later, we see Truman stop at a newstand, where he buys a newspaper and a magazine for his wife.

Out on the street, he is accosted by twins (Ron and Don). They cheerily exchange greetings. Truman reminds them about the insurance policy he is trying to sell them. He jokes about it being a 'doppelganger [double] special'.

He arrives at the front door of his office building, and happily lets fellow workers go in ahead of him. 'I'm not that anxious to get there,' he says.

12 Truman's office, day

Truman is sitting at his desk, somewhat bored. When he thinks no one is listening, he dials the phone. He is trying to get directory assistance for Fiji. He is interrupted however by a fellow worker just over the partition wall. Surreptitiously, he tries to find the number of someone called 'Garland'.

He looks at a glamour magazine which has pictures of attractive women. Covering what he is doing with a cough, he rips the last part of the image showing the models eyes out of the magazine.

His superior appears, and asks him to close an account at Wells Park, on Harbour Island. Truman pleads a dental appointment, but his supervisor warns him that he must do the job. There have been cutbacks (and Truman's job is in jeopardy). Reluctantly, Truman accepts the job.

13 Ferry jetty, Seahaven, day

Truman buys a ticket from the man in the ticket office. He walks with obvious reluctance along the jetty towards the waiting ferry. As he goes, he sees a sunken boat lying in the water. At this point, his nerve fails and he turns back. Despite the help offered by the ferry attendants, he returns to shore.

14 Truman's garden, day

Meryl arrives home, dressed in her nurse's uniform. She greets him with 'Hi, honey!'. Then she shows him a 'Chef's Pal' food peeler than she has, and gives what amounts to a mini-commercial for the item. He pronounces it 'Amazing!'

15 The unfinished Seahaven bridge, night

Truman and his friend Marlon are practising golf shots on the empty causeway. Marlon endorses a beer (which is in clear view of the camera).

Truman tells Marlon, '**You know, I'm thinking of getting out**'. He means leaving his job and getting off the island. Marlon wants to know what could be wrong with his job, which is a desk job. Marlon asks where there is to go, and Truman replies, '**Fiji**'. Marlon has never heard of it, so Truman shows him using a golf ball to represent the Earth. When Marlon asks when he is going, Truman replies, 'It takes money, and planning. You can't just up and go.' But he assures Marlon that '**I'm gonna do it**'.

16   Ocean, day (flashback)

Truman and his father are in a small sailing dinghy. The weather turns bad. Truman's father tells him, 'We should go back!'. But young Truman begs his father to go on. A storm comes on and the dinghy is swamped by waves. Truman's father is washed out of the boat, and despite the boy's attempts to save him, drops away beneath the waves.

17   Beach, night

Truman is sitting pensively on the sand. Suddenly, a shower of water falls on him from above. All around him however is dry. He jumps up and moves. The 'rain' follows him. Then the rain pours out of the night.

18   Truman's home, night

Truman comes in soaked. Meryl scolds him. He tells her about his dream of going round the world. She tells him he's talking like a teenager, and reminds him of the mortgage and car payments they have. She adds, pleadingly, 'And I thought we were going to try for a baby'. He tells her **'That can wait. I need to get away. See some of the world. Explore!'**
Meryl tells him everyone thinks like this. She is going to get him out of the wet clothes and into bed.

19   Garage office, night

Two men are watching the show. One complains that '**You never see anything**' (meaning sex on 'The Truman Show').

20   Seahaven city centre, day

Truman buys a paper and another magazine. He cheerily greets the newspaper seller.

He is walking along the street, which is full of people. Suddenly he sees a familiar face. An old derelict is staring at him.

'Dad?!' he cries and moves forward. At that moment, the old man is swept away by anonymous people and bundled onto a bus. Truman tries to get to him, but is hampered by the crowd. He bangs on the side of the bus but it drives off, leaving Truman standing, confused, in the middle of the road. The storm of activity dissipates and all is calm again.

21   Truman's mother's house, day

Truman's mother is explaining that she often sees men she thinks are his father. Truman declares that the 'homeless man' *was* his lost father. He was amazed at the way people came out of nowhere and forced him onto the bus. His mother can only express relief at having such people removed. Truman protests that they never found his father's body. He asks if there was a brother. She reminds him that his father was an only child, like him. She goes on, telling him 'I never blamed you, Truman' [about urging his father to go off into the storm].

22   Truman's basement, night

Truman unlocks a trunk and looks furtively through the memorabilia inside, including an old photograph of his father. Just at that moment, he is interrupted by Meryl, who has come to find him. He tells her '**I saw my father today**'. She gently rebukes him for upsetting his mother. When it is obvious that he is in a strange mood, she changes the subject. He handles a red cardigan.

23   Bar, night

A waitress comments that though they got rid of her (the actress who wore the cardigan) they couldn't erase the memory.

24   College sports field, day (flashback)

A younger version of Truman is at a college game. He looks across and sees an attractive young woman (Sylvia), who smiles at him. Just then, Meryl stumbles into him (accidentally on purpose) and they meet. He is distracted. When he looks back, Sylvia has gone.

25   College dance (flashback)

Truman is dancing with Meryl, who is doing her best to keep his attention. However, he spots 'Lauren' (Sylvia), dancing with someone else. They exchange meaningful glances. Suddenly, men come and take Sylvia away (against her will). Truman cannot prevent it.

26   College library (flashback)

Truman is working on his college studies. Meryl and Marlon are trying to get him to come with them, but he resists their temptations. They go. Left alone, he notices the hand of the female student in the desk opposite – and the bracelet that 'Lauren'

(Sylvia) was wearing at the dance. He looks over the desk and makes conversation with her. 'Lauren' warns him, '**Look…I'm not allowed to talk to you**'. He persists and asks her out, some time. She writes 'NOW', adding 'If we don't go now, we won't have the chance'. They leave the library, to the dismay of someone who was obviously watching them.

27   Beach, day (flashback)

Truman leads 'Lauren' (Sylvia) down to the water's edge. She takes off her cardigan. She is excited, but tells him 'They're going to be here any minute… **They don't want me talking to you**'. They kiss. Truman, curious, asks what 'they' want. She replies urgently, **Listen to me. Everyone knows about…everything you do. Cause they're pretending, Truman. Do you…understand? Everyone's pretending.**

She tells him that her name is not Lauren, but Sylvia. At that moment, a car roars onto the beach and a man gets out. He tells Truman he is Lauren's father, though she protests that she has never seen him before. The man 'explains' that Lauren is schizophrenic. He bundles her into the car, against her will. He tells Truman they are going away, to Fiji. The car roars off again. Truman is left with nothing but Sylvia's red cardigan.

28   Bar, night

One waitress asks the other why he didn't just follow her (Sylvia) to Fiji, but is told that his mother got sick and he couldn't leave her (his mother). Then he married Meryl 'on the rebound'. The boss grumbles, 'You've already got this [scene] on the 'Greatest Hits' tape!'

29   Truman's basement, night

Truman is brooding over the red cardigan. He picks up a framed photo of Meryl and opens the back of the frame. Inside is hidden his 'identikit' image of Sylvia.

30   Sylvia's apartment, day

We see Sylvia, on the point of crying, watching the broadcast as Truman attempts to reassemble the elements of her face.

31   Truman's car, day

Truman is driving to work, listening to the radio. The reception is faulty, so he fiddles with the set. Suddenly, he hears transmissions from a completely different source – and realises that they are talking about his movements. Then the voice tells everyone to change frequencies. There is a terrible squeal (of noise feedback) and all the extras in the Seahaven square wince (the noise is in their earpieces). The radio program comes back on.

32   Omnicom office building, day

Truman doesn't go on his usual route. He walks a different way, then sits down, brooding. Suddenly he makes his way into another building. Security guards look at him anxiously. He gets into a lift, and sees that it is a fake – there is no rear wall, and he can see 'extras' in a room out the back. At this moment, the guards grab him and forcibly evict him from the building.

33   Mini-market

Truman finds Marlon, who is stocking a vending machine. He whispers anxiously to Marlon, **'I'm on to something, Marlon'**. He tries to explain that **'strange things have been happening'**, mentioning the false elevator and the radio transmissions. He tells Marlon he thinks it's about 'my Dad'. He points to the people in the store, and claps his hands. They don't react at all. He urges Marlon to come with him.

34   Beach, sunset

Truman tries to explain to Marlon that he feels that 'your whole life has been building towards something'. Marlon admires the sunset. Truman tells him that he's going away.

35   Truman's house, day

Truman is sitting with Meryl and his mother, looking at a photo album. His mother is cooing over pictures of Truman as a baby and small boy. There is a picture of them at Mt. Rushmore (the huge carved mountain monument). Truman, startled, remarks that **'It's so small'** (and the picture confirms that it is a 'mini Mt. Rushmore). His mother turns the page quickly and tells him that things always look small. Meryl comments lovingly on the photos of their wedding day. Truman's mother drops hints about wanting to have a grandchild. Meryl and Truman's mother go out, leaving Truman in front of the television. Suddenly Truman notices that in the wedding photo Meryl has her fingers crossed.

36   Truman's house, day

The sun comes up (in 'fast forward'). Truman wants to talk to Meryl. She however is evasive, saying she has to go to the hospital. She tells him she is needed in surgery, but appears flustered, as if she is making up the details. Truman slyly says, as she goes out, 'I'll cross my fingers for you'.

When Meryl leaves on her bicycle, Truman grabs his bike and pedals off after her.

37   Hospital, day

Truman is pursuing Meryl when he is stopped by a receptionist, who tells him he can't see Meryl. He asks her to pass on a message: '**I had to go to Fiji, and that I'll call her when I get there**'. The receptionist goes off. Truman again tries to follow Meryl. He is blocked several times, but makes it to the operating theatre, where he looks through the window and sees Meryl assisting a surgeon. At that moment, a security guard pulls down the blind on the window. Inside, out of sight of Truman, the 'surgeon' abandons the 'operation'.

38   Travel agency, day

Truman asks the woman to book a flight to Fiji. She checks the computer, and announces that there is no booking for a month. He tells her that he will make other arrangements.

39   Bus station, day

Truman boards the bus for Chicago. It is full of passengers. One little girl recognises him, but her mother shushes her. The driver grinds the gears and there is a terrible noise. Then he announces that there is a mechanical problem. All the passengers leave the bus.

40   Bar, night

The waitress and bartender are discussing Truman's interest in Chicago. She tells him that he 'has to have it out with Meryl'.

41   Truman's car, day

Truman is sitting in his car, waiting. Meryl appears. He urges her to get in. He points out to her how a lady on a bike, a man with flowers and a VW beetle regularly 'loop' past. Meryl tries to distract him by mentioning a barbecue. She tells him he's upset because of wanting to go to Fiji, and promises to go in a few months time. He replies, 'Let's go now'.

He drives at speed round a roundabout, telling her gleefully, '**I guess we're being spontaneous**'. He heads off, but the street is suddenly jammed with vehicles. He reverses, and announces that he wants to go to New Orleans. As he drives up the road which was jammed, he points out to her, 'Same road, no cars. It's magic'. He heads off.

42   Bridge out of Seahaven, day

They have arrived at the bridge, and Truman is frozen with fear (at crossing water). She urges him, '**Let's go home where you'll feel safe**'. But he puts her hand on the steering wheel, closes his eyes and accelerates onto the bridge. Meryl screams, but has no choice but to steer. Shortly, they are over the bridge. He is jubilant.

43   Road outside Seahaven, day

They are on the open road. A sign warns about a fire hazard. Truman takes no notice and drives on. A wall of fire appears, right across the road. Truman drives straight through it. They emerge on the other side. Truman is excited.

Meryl asks how they are going to pay for the trip to New Orleans, and protests that they will eat into their savings, and that his mother will be 'worried sick'. Truman takes no notice.

They come upon a crowd of emergency personnel and vehicles. A sign announces a leak at a nuclear power plant. A policeman stops Truman and tells him that the whole area has been evacuated. Finally, defeated, Truman accepts that he can't go on. He thanks the policeman, who unwittingly replies, '**You're welcome, Truman**'. Truman understands the significance of this slip. He jumps from the car, and runs.

44   Forest, day

Truman is trying to get away, but he is surrounded by men in silver radiation suits. They pin him to the ground.

45   Truman's home, day

Two policemen have delivered Truman home. Meryl thanks them.
Truman is sitting gloomily, looking on.

Suddenly he asks her, '**Why do you want to have a baby with
me? You can't stand me.**' Meryl, shocked, suggests a cocoa drink
and launches into a testimonial. Truman snaps, '**Who are you
talking to?**' He accuses her of being part of 'this' (the whole
setup). She picks up some kitchen implements and holds them out
as if to ward him off. Truman circles her. She blurts out, 'Do something!' Truman seizes on this, asking her who she is talking to.
She denies she said anything and tries to escape.

There is a knock at the door. Marlon enters. Meryl rushes to
him, and collapses into his arms, saying, '**Oh my God. How can
anyone expect me to carry on under these conditions? It's
unprofessional!**' Marlon comforts her, while Truman looks on.

46   Unfinished bridge, night

Truman and Marlon are sitting on their cars. Truman admits that
he might be losing his mind. He adds, '**it's like the whole world
revolves around me somehow**'. Marlon tells him he's imagining it.
He reminds Truman that they have been best friends since childhood, and recalls amusing moments. He tells Truman that 'You're
the closest thing I've ever had to a brother'.

47   Studio control room

We see Cristof speaking into his headset, saying, 'The point is,
I'd gladly walk in front of traffic for you'. On the studio monitor,
we see Marlon saying to Truman, '**The point is, I'd gladly step in
front of traffic for you, Truman.**' Cristof adds, '**And the last thing
I'd ever do is lie to you**'.

48   Bridge, night

Marlon says, with the greatest sincerity, 'And the last thing I'd
ever do is lie to you.'

At this moment, Marlon announces that 'You were right about
one thing'. Truman sees a shadowy figure approaching. It is his
father. Marlon says, 'Go to him'.

49   Control room

Cristof tells the crew, 'Easy on the fog' and cues the crane cam, and then the 'button cam'.

50   Bridge, night

Truman has gone to meet his father, saying 'I never stopped believing'. We meanwhile see 'cutaways' to the people in the bar and two old ladies watching the show at home.

51   Control room

Cristof controls the cameras being used to shoot the reunion scene.

52   Bridge, night

Truman and his father embrace.

53   Control room

Cristof orders music and a close up.

54   Bridge, night

The reunion is played out with great emotion. We cut away to the control room, to the bar, to the old ladies and some Japanese viewers – all embracing, jubilant at the emotional scene.

55   Control room

There is wild excitement and people congratulate Cristof on his brilliance (at orchestrating the reunion scene). Someone says, '**Great television!**'.

56   Sylvia's apartment, night

Sylvia, morose, has watched the reunion scene too. She however understands how fake it is.

57   TV set

We see Truman on TV (the set itself is visible) drinking chocolate as an advertising 'crawler' runs across the bottom of the screen. We cut away to Sylvia, sadly watching Truman on TV. An announcer sums up the Truman phenomenon as we see a montage of significant moments in Truman's life. We see shots of various locations where the show is broadcast, including Times Square (New York) and giant outdoor viewing event (with Truman's marriage on huge screens). The announcer describes the international audience that watched Truman's birth and followed his every move. He refers to Seahaven island, enclosed in 'the largest studio ever constructed', so big that it's visible from space (as we see a pullback shot that reveals the sheer size of the studio dome) and ends triumphantly on 'It's The Truman Show!'.

A TV presenter (Mike) welcomes viewers to 'Tru Talk' – a show about 'The Truman Show'. We see cutaway shots to various audience members watching. As we zoom in to the 'moon' above Seahaven, and see Cristof inside, Mike introduces 'the world's greatest televisionary… architect of the world within a world…Cristof'.

58   Lunar room

Cristof sits and is interviewed. He admits that the attempt of Truman's father to infiltrate the show has prompted the 'recent dramatic events', and concedes that it 'is not the first time that someone from the outside has attempted to reach Truman'.

59   Truman's house, day (flashback)

A young man leaps from a gift box, and cries, 'I did it! I'm on the Truman Show!' We also see a shot of a man parachuting into the street behind Truman with a sign reading 'TRUMAN YOU ARE ON TV'.

60   Lunar room

Cristof goes on that since 'Kirk' (Truman's father) started the crisis, 'he was the only one who could end it'.

61   Beach (flashback)

We see Kirk holding back the boy Truman, who is trying to climb a rock wall to see what is on the other side.

62   Lunar room

Cristof explains that the father was 'written out' (of the show) because it was necessary to 'manufacture ways to keep him [Truman] on the island'.

63 School (flashback)

The boy Truman informs his teacher that he wants to be an explorer. She pulls down the map of the world and tells him, 'There's nothing left to explore'.

64 Lunar room

Cristof explains how he tried to find ways of keeping Truman on the island. We see a savage dog barking at young Truman (in flashback). Finally Cristof came up with the concept of Kirk being drowned at sea (Scene 16), causing Truman to be terrified of water. He has explained Kirk's absence as due to amnesia.

Cristof takes callers. One asks about the number of cameras in Seahaven. The answer is 5000. They started with one, when Truman was born. (We cut to vision of Truman as a foetus, then as a baby – followed by shots of Truman as a child.) Truman was the first of five unwanted pregnancies to be born on the date the show was due to go to air for the first time. He was legally adopted by the (TV) corporation. The show generates 'enormous revenues', without commercial interruption, by 'product placement'. Everything on the show is for sale and available from a 'Truman Catalog'. We see cutaway shots showing the various product lines, and users of the products. Cristof explains Truman's ignorance of the illusion because 'We accept the reality of the world with which we're presented'. Another caller rings in, from Hollywood.

65 Sylvia's apartment, night

This time it is Sylvia. We cut to her room and see her angrily talking on the phone. She accuses Cristof:

> Quote
>
> You're a liar and a manipulator and what you've done to Truman is sick.

We cut back to the Lunar Room, and then back and forth to Sylvia's apartment during the rest of the scene. Cristof recognises her, and patronisingly tells her she has no right to judge. He retorts:

> Quote
>
> I have given Truman the chance to live a normal life. The world – the place you live in – is the sick place. Seahaven is the way the world should be.

He adds that Truman 'prefers his "cell", as you call it'. He ends the interview, adding that Meryl will be leaving Truman in an upcoming episode. He also mentions that he is determined to have '**television's first on air conception**' very soon. We see Sylvia, looking longingly and sadly at Truman on the TV.

65   Control room

It is night. Cristof is looking thoughtfully at the sleeping Truman on a giant screen. He reaches out and touches the image of Truman.

The sun comes up in Seahaven. Truman is in the bathroom. We see his image (as shot by the hidden camera behind the bathroom mirror). Two technicians are watching Truman, watching them. '**Come in Major Burbank**,' he says into the mirror. He draws a face with the soap on the mirror, and comments '**that one's for free**'.

66   Truman's home, exterior, day

Truman comes out of his front door and does his 'Good Morning, Good Evening and Goodnight' exchange with his neighbours.

67   Japanese home

A Japanese family repeat this formula (practising their English).

68   Truman's home, exterior, day

Truman has his formula encounter with Spencer and his dog.

69   Seahaven street, day

Truman has his formula encounter with the twins. They announce that they are going to sign up for a policy.

70   Truman's office, day

Truman is on the phone, talking in a joking fashion about insurance when a new female worker (Vivian) is introduced to him (obviously the replacement for Meryl).

71   Control room

We see Truman mowing the lawn. The technicians are watching the monitors of Truman's house. Cristof comes in and asks what is happening. The scene in Truman's basement. Nothing is happening. They report that Truman has been there since Meryl left. Cristof, suspicious, asks them to check for breathing.

72   Garage security room
The guards are discussing what is happening.

73   Control room
They are watching a playback of the most recent shots of Truman. Cristof orders one of the technicians to zoom in on Truman. There is a shot of a hand. Cristof orders Marlon to be called. We cut to a shot of Marlon roaring through the streets of Seahaven in his pickup truck.

74   Truman's basement
Marlon climbs down into the basement, calling out to Truman. There is no answer. He uncovers the 'body' and it is a blow up toy. Cristof (aware that all this is being televised live) tells him to 'Keep it light'. Cristof is watching all this desperately. Marlon uncovers a set of steps leading up to a concealed trapdoor. Cristof orders the technicians to bring up the 'lawn cam'.

75   Truman's garden, night
Marlon pops up through the trapdoor into Truman's lawn. 'He's gone!' says Marlon.

76   Control room
Cristof orders them to cut transmission (of the show).

77   Bar, night
There is consternation when the picture goes. We cut to the old ladies, who wake up to find that the show is not on.

78   Control room
There is consternation in the control room. A search is organised. Cristof, beside himself, tells them '**He has the world's most recognisable face…he can't disappear**'.

79   Street, night
The cast of 'The Truman Show' (the actors playing the townspeople) are methodically searching for Truman.

80   Control room
Cristof is anxiously directing the search.

81   Bridge, day
The twins have dropped their pretence of niceness, and are angry that the 'sonofabitch' has escaped.

82   Control room
Cristof, desperate because the searching is so difficult, calls out to 'Cue the sun!'

83   Seahaven, day
The sun comes up – to the amazement of the cast.

84   Control room
A network executive comes in, anxious about rumours Truman is dead and that sponsors are going to rip up their contracts.

85   Seahaven, day
The cast are in their 'first positions', waiting for Truman.

86   Control room
Cristof suddenly realises that they aren't watching the sea. He calls up the sea camera. They find Truman and resume transmission. We cut away to the bar, where the viewers are making bets about whether Truman will get away.

87   Truman's boat, day
We see Truman in the *Santa Maria*, sailing across the 'sea'. He is looking at his final 'identikit' picture of Sylvia, which he has taken with him on his escape. We cut away to Sylvia, who is watching this moment emotionally.

88   Control room
Cristof orders a boat to go after Truman.

89   Seahaven ferry, day
The ferry captain is the same actor as the bus driver, and doesn't know a thing about piloting a boat.

90   Control room

Cristof orders the use of the weather program. The operators are worried, but Cristof tells them that he'll turn back because he'll be too afraid.

91   Truman's boat, day

The 'storm' breaks over the *Santa Maria*. Truman clings to the boat as it pitches on the waves. We cut away to the man in the bathtub, watching every moment. He calls out (to Truman), 'You can do it! Hold on!'

Truman calls out, '**Is that the best you can do? You're gonna have to kill me!**' He sings a sea shanty.

92   Control room

Cristof orders the wind up – then adds 'Capsize him!' The others are horrified. One notes, 'He's gonna drown and he doesn't even care'. They watch the storm. We cut back to Truman and his attempts to survive the storm. Finally Cristof tells them to stop the storm.

93   Truman's boat, day

Truman hauls himself upright. He sails on. Later, we see him sailing across the mirror smooth water. Suddenly, the boat stops. It has hit something. Truman climbs forward. The boat has hit the wall (of the studio). He slaps the wall in frustration. Then he climbs out of the boat and carefully walks along the wall. He comes to a set of stairs and the exit door. He opens the door.

94   Control room

Cristof puts on the speaker, and addresses Truman directly (from the sky). When Truman asks who he is, Cristof says 'I am the creator of a television show that gives hope and joy and inspiration to millions'. He tells Truman he is the star. Truman asks if anything was real.

Quote

You were real. That's what made you so good to watch. Listen to me, Truman. There's no more truth out there than there is in the world I created for you. Same lies. The same deceit. But in my world, you have nothing to fear. I know you better than you know yourself.

Truman denies this. Cristof tells him he can't leave. He recalls how he (Cristof) saw every important moment of Truman's life. When Truman is silent, Cristof orders him to say something: '**You're on television. You're live to the whole world!**'

95   *Sylvia's apartment*
We have cut to Sylvia, who has been watching the telecast, anxiously cheering Truman on, saying '**Do it!**'.

96   *Sea wall, day*
Truman bows deeply, says '**In case I don't see you, good afternoon, good evening and goodnight**'. He climbs through the exit door and disappears.

97   *Sylvia's apartment, day*
We cut back to Sylvia, running down the stairs (on her way to meet him).

98   *Various locations*
Viewers everywhere erupt in joy when they see what Truman has done.

99   *Control room*
While Cristof looks on stunned, the network executive orders the technicians to close down the show. The screen goes blank.

100   *Security office*
The two guards have been watching all this. Bored, one asks the other what else is on television.

The Text and What it Says About *Image*

What sort of text is this?

The Truman Show is what theorists call a 'self-reflexive' text. That is, it reflects on itself. Think of a mirror. It reflects whatever is in front of it – for example, you. This movie is about its subject – Truman – but it is also about the whole process of representing 'reality' in images.

Satire

It is also, and most importantly, a satire. It offers a critique of the way the media manipulate us, and the way we participate in the media as willing spectators (by way of escapism, voyeurism and identification or vicarious experience). It asks us to think about how much we can trust television, even shows which are supposedly 'real' – and also how much we have made the simulated 'reality' of television (and movies) part of our lives.

Genres

Specifically, in terms of its media satire, it critiques three well known genres: documentaries, popular American soap operas or sitcoms and 'reality TV'.

Documentary

The first genre type is documentary. Think of the beginning of the film, where three principal participants (who are all fictional, remember) talk to the audience directly – looking into the camera lens. They appear to be telling us 'the truth'. Yet the film undercuts their remarks – for the rest of the story establishes quite clearly that their claim to authenticity is false. Truman's life is *not* 'all real' and the assertion that 'there's nothing fake' about the show is ludicrous. The authenticity they speak of is bogus. What is the nett effect of such undercutting? To make us analyse the whole idea of representations made on TV. Who is telling the truth? Who is lying? How much can we trust what media people say?

Soap opera / sitcom

The second genre type may not be immediately obvious, but think about the way it represents its characters. Everyone lives in a picture-perfect town called Seahaven, the sort of idyllic American town Walt Disney would have built. In this 'perfect' town, all the streets are clean, the lawns are cut, people smile and all is sweetness and light. Look at Meryl's hair – blond and perfectly coiffed.

Think of the names of the bridesmaids – Jodie, Jean and Joanne – of the wedding photos, the childhood album, and so on. In most traditional (particularly 1950s, 1960s, 1970s and 1980s) sitcoms or soapies, everyone is beautiful. They live in picture perfect places. In sitcoms they are terribly nice, terribly tolerant, terribly wise, and all problems are solved by the final scene of each episode. In soapies, they are not all terribly nice, but they are all beautiful and live luxurious lives. Classic examples might be *Father Knows Best* (1950s), *Mr Ed* (1960s), *I Dream of Jeannie* (1960s), *The Cosby Show* (1980s), *Friends* (1990s).

Reality TV

The third genre that comes in for a serve is 'reality TV'. Ironically, since this movie was made in 1998, the genre has only got more and more extreme. *The Truman Show* anticipates the worst excesses of *The Bachelor* or *Survivor* in a way which was remarkably prescient. (Of that, more below.)

How is the text constructed?

Consider the extraordinary construction of the movie – rather like a set of Russian dolls, one element embedded within another.

The show within the show

Inside the film (one conceptual framework) called *The Truman Show* is a TV program (another conceptual framework) also called 'The Truman Show'. The first (the movie) is about the second (the TV show), but also invites you to think about the film itself (ie it reflects on itself). 'Inside' the movie, as well as the TV show itself, there are also the 'behind the scenes' scenes – those shot in the 'Lunar Room' and the control room. These are outside 'The Truman Show' (which is a narrative) but inside *The Truman Show* (the narrative about a narrative). Also inside the movie, but outside the TV program, is the 'Tru Talk' show (57-64) – a show about the show within the movie. And also outside 'The Truman Show' but inside the movie is the audience of 'The Truman Show' (glimpsed in a number of 'cutaway' or 'reaction' scenes, including, very obviously, the final scene of the whole film), and these are a separate element again. They are watching Truman, who is also watched by Cristof, and all three are watched by us. It is a little like standing between two mirrors, and seeing ourselves reflected not once, but many times. It is a remarkable text in its complexity.

(I) Truman Show Film

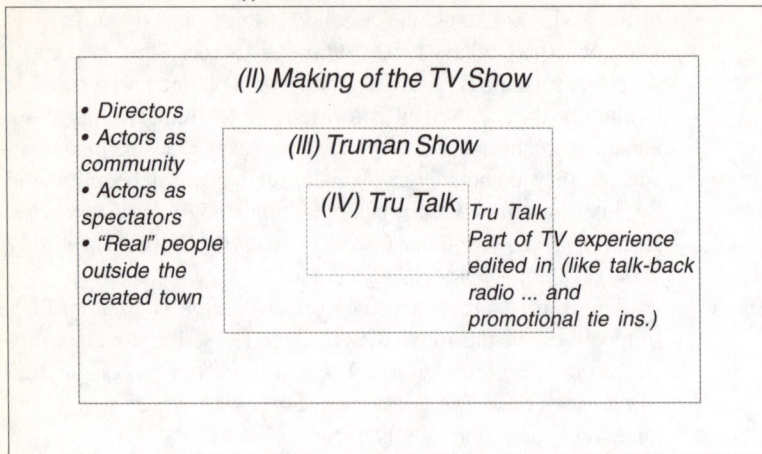

(II) Making of the TV Show

- Directors
- Actors as community
- Actors as spectators
- "Real" people outside the created town

(III) Truman Show

(IV) Tru Talk

Tru Talk
Part of TV experience edited in (like talk-back radio ... and promotional tie ins.)

Film spectators (US)

How does the text comment on 'reality'?

Simulation

What of 'reality'? The first thing to be said about the movie is that it is fiction – ie, not 'real'. Yet everyone who watches it recognises how neatly it satirises the whole 'reality TV' trend (see notes below), as well as the notion of spectatorship and celebrity worship. So it is a simulation (and exaggeration) of 'reality' – just like the shows it is mocking and critiquing. It 'represents' a part of the real world ('reality') in an exaggerated form. Theorists have

'Hyper-reality'

called this 'hyperreality' – meaning experiencing a virtual or simulated reality (interacting with it as if it were real, though knowing it is constructed). Disneyland (and a good many less spectacular theme parks) is a perfect example. It simulates or represents the 'real' in such a way as people can enjoy the experience, while knowing it is 'fake'. So are glamorous shopping centres with false gardens and fountains, or fake Irish pubs, or for that matter fake Aussie outback pubs. Truman is in a fake world, which he takes for a real world. In this illusion is satirised our tendency

Representa-
tion and
reality

to confuse the two. The *representation* and the *real* are different things, yet *The Truman Show* shows how the media confuse them, to the point where people don't know any more what is real and what is constructed. In doing this it asks us to think long and hard about how accurate all representations of reality are.

Clearly Truman's life is completely 'set up' for the consumption of the TV audience, in very much the way a real life show like *Big Brother* or *Survivor* sets up an experiment in 'reality' for the pleasure of viewers. Cristof famously says 'there's nothing fake about The Truman Show' and Marlon adds 'It's all real' – but Weir invites us (as critical viewers) to dissent from these claims.

Fake products

It's rather like passing off a fake Rolex watch picked up somewhere in Asia as a real Rolex watch. The two look the same, but one is genuine and one is a forgery. However, what if someone gave you the fake Rolex and you actually thought it was the genuine article. Would it not please you? If subjectively (in your mind) it *was* 'real', then its objective falsity would not count. In somewhat the same way, Weir asks us to consider this sort of question in relation to media representations: if it looks real, and the people involved think it's real, maybe it is (for them) 'real'. So are the media manipulators really 'faking', or just constructing their own 'reality'?

What is the text saying about the media?

The illusion of TV and film

The Truman Show is a brilliant exposé of the **illusion** (the 'construction' of 'reality') wrapped up in the process of making film and TV products. We all know it happens, but rarely is it so dramatically exposed. Let's consider some examples:

• **Set design** as illusion (the lift scene, 31, and the final sailing sequences with the cyclorama wall that Truman's boat crashes into are the clearest examples)

• **Special effects** – such as fire (the road out of Seahaven), rain (17), the storm at sea (16, 91-92) and especially 'sunrise' (83)

• **Dialogue** – the illusion being that this is what people really say of their own volition – critiqued memorably in Scenes 47-48, when Cristof cues 'spontaneous' dialogue for Marlon

• **Editing** and **'composition'** – as in Scene 49, when Cristof cues the fake fog, the music, and so on, to create the desired (emotional) effect

• **Music** – as in the father and son reunion scene (53)

• **Actors and extras** – as in the command 'Stand by all extras' in Scene 31 and 'Position 1' in Scene 85, not to mention Truman's own exposure (Scene 41) of the 'loops' that he has noticed (the woman on the bicycle, the VW, etc)

• **Camera positions** – as in the 'lens' shots of Truman in the bathroom (2, 4, 8), the dashboard camera shot in Scene 31, the crane shot in Scenes 41(Truman driving in circles) and 49 (reunion).

The film goes beyond merely exposing cinematic trickery. It actually draws our attention as well to filmic conventions – the standard ways of doing things visually. Examples are the significant objects which occur at several times in the story – the bracelet of the girl Truman is keen on, the red cardigan (a memento of his 'lost love'), the crossed fingers in the wedding photo, the childhood treasures in Truman's basement trunk, etc. Another convention is that of 'buddies' (we would say 'mates'), as in the recurring talks of Truman and Marlon.

What is the text saying about the act of viewing images?

Spectatorship As well as revealing the illusions behind the real-seeming façade of TV and cinema, the movie also has quite a lot to say about 'spectatorship' – the actual act of viewing. The satire, let us note, is *not* just of the media. It is also a comment on *us*, the consumers of images.

Why people watch Consider the first shot in which the garage attendants appear (19). 'You never get to see anything,' says one, irritably, referring to explicit images of sex (or the lack thereof). What does this say about him (and presumably his mate)? That he watches reality TV in the hope of a sexual turn on. Later, we see the waitresses participating emotionally in Truman's love life (28), and understand that they are living vicariously through the mediated (represented) images of another person's life. Then there are the Japanese who use the show to learn English, the old ladies who fill their time and an emotional vacuum in their lives with a televisual 'family' (or relationships), the man in the bath who wants to identify with the 'hero' Truman (who, we guess, compensates for the man's own lack of heroism). And the movie ends, most significantly, with the garage attendants. Once Truman is off the air, they look around, bored, for some other form of mediated stimulation. 'What else is on?' So TV is just a 'hit' of stimulation, something to look at. There is no personal engagement. It is just moving wallpaper.

Weir (and Niccol) are not condemning the act of viewing –

The film's judgement

though they *do* express an implicit concern about the quality of some viewers (such as the garage men). But they are showing that viewers are *complicit* in the act of media consumption. They are *willing spectators*. Without such spectators, there would be no media circus. The illusions, the fake reality, is there to satisfy a demand. It's a transaction, and to condemn the producers and media manipulators is to only see half the story. They are giving people what they want. The question must also be asked, in fairness: Why do people like looking at other people? Why is 'voyeurism' so popular? Is this a good or bad thing, or neither – just human nature?

What is the text saying about the uses of mediated images?

Why do people watch the media

Some of the most cutting satire in *The Truman Show* has to do with how images are used by the media. To simplify somewhat, we could say that there are three broad purposes for the construction of 'reality' (as exemplified in 'The Truman Show'):

(1)   The satisfaction of a demand for voyeurism and narrative

The desire to look at pretty objects

We have already considered the idea that people *like* looking at other people. The media satisfy this demand by providing such images. Needless to say, they 'idealise' the images to make them more pleasing – exactly as a dish in a classy restaurant is enhanced to make it more attractive to the consumer – or a newsreader or reporter (especially a woman one) is as attractive as possible. So viewers tune in to see nice looking Truman Burbank and his attractive wife in their lovely house in their beautiful town – and *enjoy looking at them*.

The desire for 'story'

Even more sophisticated is the satisfaction of people's demand for 'story'. So viewers tune in to see what will happen next. One clear example is the 'drowning' of Kirk Burbank, and the attendant grief (referred to in Scene 21), and another is when Cristof tells viewers that Meryl will shortly leave Truman, but that Truman will still become a father in the very first 'on air conception'. This could be called the ultimate narrative hook – the reason for tuning in par excellence.

(2) The transmission of cultural paradigms

*How the
media
reinforce
cultural
norms*

It is hard to argue that all media people have a conscious agenda of cultural transmission – in other words that they deliberately set out with the intention of moulding people's opinions and providing guides for behaviour or belief. Some do, no doubt, but how many? What is much more likely is that they bow to the dominant forces in a society because that is going to be most acceptable to their viewers. They reflect and mimic dominant patterns, rather than going *against* them. So, for instance, they show images of heterosexual love (conventional romances), of the predominant racial types (shows dominated by 'white' people), of the prevailing belief systems (morally affirmative cop shows and patriotic action movies) and so on, and largely stay away from controversial issues and minority images.

Media commentators have long argued however that this has the effect of reinforcing the dominant values in a community. So seeing images of 'straight' people all the time has the effect of marginalising gay people. Seeing whites all the time has the effect of making blacks seem different. Seeing pretty girls everywhere has the effect of making plain girls feel bad. And so it goes. In *The Truman Show*, Meryl, for instance, is a fascinating glimpse of the 'all American wife' stereotype – blond, blue-eyed, domesticated, submissive, obsessed with gadgets and food. Imagine what feminists would make of her in a serious cultural analysis.

(3) The commercial exploitation of the viewers (who are consumers)

*Product
placement*

A subtheme that the movie advances quite clearly is how the media tie in with commercial interests. Once again, *The Truman Show* was ahead of its time. 'Product placement' has become a stock in trade of filmmakers. Think of James Bond and BMW cars or the way Budweiser seems to appear in so many American movies. This is no accident. The manufacturers have paid for their products to appear, seeing it (rightly) as subliminal advertising. An interesting and important variation is commercial 'tie ins' or merchandising. Remember the number of Harry Potter products that appeared every time a new film came out? Seeing the movie leads the consumer to buy the products tied in to the movie.

The Truman Show pins this down exactly. Meryl essentially gives advertising pitches for products (Scenes 14 and 45). Marlon endorses a type of beer (15). Truman likes a particular type of chocolate. And in Scene 64, we learn that you can buy anything on the show – clothes, houses, appliances – from *The Truman Catalog* – the ultimate in merchandising.

Media manipulation

Weir and Niccol are reminding us how easily we are manipulated by advertisers. Although Cristof justifies the practice (64), because it helps pay for this expensive show in a discreet way, it raises some big questions about how controlled we are, and whether the media are not an arm of capitalism or manufacturing, when an arm's length distance (leaving them to just entertain) might be rather safer.

What is the text saying about how we should regard the media?

What comment are Weir and Niccol making? One commentary put it rather neatly:

> Quote

> The fake landscape Truman lives in is our own media landscape in which news, politics, advertising and public affairs are increasingly made up of theatrical illusions....It is convincing in its realism, with lifelike simulations and story lines, from the high-tech facsimile of a sun that benevolently beams down on Truman to the mock sincerity of the actor he mistakenly believes is his best friend...Truman's fear of leaving this invented world, once he realises it is a fraud, is similarly like our own reluctance to break our symbiotic relationship with media....And the producer-director of this stage-set world, who blocks Truman's effort to escape, is the giant media companies, news organisations, and media-politicians that have a stake in keeping us surrounded by falsehood, and are prepared to lure us with rewards as they block efforts at reforming the system.

In short, the movie is a fiction with a serious point to make about reality. We cannot resist the media, who offer us images of the real world (as well as fantasy and imagination). We have little choice but to trust much of what they show us – because we have no alternative view. And because of their cunning, we enjoy the chance to view their images of reality. But at the same time, we suspect that they are manipulating us, for good or ill.

In Truman we have an extreme (and fictitious) example of media manipulation. Let us not overlook the fact however that Truman ultimately rebels, claims back his own life, and defies the seduction of the media. In this he is a kind of model for us, a character who embodies the critical thinking and individualism which is necessary if we are to avoid being the helpless creatures of others.

Related Texts

The real 'reality TV' shows

The Truman Show is a satire on 'reality TV'. When the movie was made in 1998, the genre was still in its infancy, but since then it has blossomed.

Precursors

For many years, television has experimented with the idea of putting real people (not actors playing characters) in dramatic situations where they are forced to react strongly. An example is the long running series *This is Your Life*, purportedly a review of a person's life story, but usually involving highly emotional reunions, which cause everyone involved to react 'live' in an unpredictable way. Daytime TV shows which specialise in the airing of real people's 'dirty laundry' (Jenny Jones, Jerry Springer and suchlike) have been around for some time and they do similar things, though their lack of any 'respectable' reason for doing so makes them much more open to criticism.

The notion of hidden cameras spying on people is itself as old as the hit series of the 1960s, *Candid Camera*. This involved people being 'set up' in a contrived situation – such as an actor misbehaving grotesquely on a street, and watching what spectators (who didn't know it was all a set up) did as they were being secretly filmed by a hidden camera. The show always ended with the 'victim' being told 'Smile, you're on Candid Camera'. So successful was this show that the phrase has gone into the popular vernacular. Other shows early in the history of TV forced contestants to do revolting things, like eating maggots, while the cameras rolled. Game shows like the Japanese ones where contestants are forced to suffer incredible torments to be in the competition for a prize are more modern developments of the same thing. The modern show, *Punk'd*, is a variation on *Candid Camera*, where a 'celebrity' is deliberately placed in an embarrassing and unpredictable situation and his/her reaction filmed.

Then there are shows which use unscripted mistakes or accidents caught accidentally on camera. This includes *Australia's Funniest Home Video Show* (based on the US original), and endless 'Bloopers' or 'Greatest Outtakes' specials which regularly screen. Another variation is the type of show that shows real footage from police cars and helicopters (as in *Cops*) or surveillance cameras of people committing crimes. These are fragments of 'real life' edited together in a sensational manner, with or without morally outraged and justifying commentary, for the voyeuristic pleasure of the viewers.

Reality TV

Reality TV in the sense of an artificial setting with real people left to their own devices really took off with *Big Brother*, the TV hit first aired in 2001. It put a group of people, equal numbers of males and females, in a closed house, and through a set of closed circuit TV cameras watched to see what they did. This was later refined in a series of variants, including shows where people had to share a flat with obnoxious individuals, or had to compete with one another in renovating a house, and so on. The common element is that the producers construct a situation with high drama potential – such as people who are bound to hate one another, or where vicious competition and betrayal are built in – and then let the largely unscripted drama play out on camera.

How it works

Reality TV is usually a compromise between scripted movie-style drama and the spectacle of 'events as they happen'. The illusion of 'real life' is provided through camera surveillance, either fixed as with *Big Brother*, or with live crews and hand-held digicams as with *Survivor*, or a hybrid approach (with some studio multi-camera work and some hand-held roaming eye footage) as with *The Bachelor*. The genre is based on the paradox that the 'real' (the initial situation) is 'constructed' (set up specially), as the audience knows, but which they willingly forget as the cunningly shaped drama of relationships and/or events unfold. In short, 'reality TV' emulates all fiction in that it pretends to be real, and the audience immerses itself in this simulated reality as if it were genuine.

You might like to refer to one or more of the following well known examples of the genre in your work:

Major examples of 'reality TV'

• ***Big Brother*** – named after the total surveillance regime of Orwell's *1984*, this hugely successful reality/game show imposed 24 hours a day surveillance on the participants, who were confined in a complex with fixed cameras in every room. The players were required to carry out tasks or challenges, and their reactions, as well as their developing relationships, recorded. The most dramatic moments of each day were then broadcast on TV. The audience was invited to nominate and vote on players, and evict individuals from the game. Product placement, as for example a game requiring use of a brand of batteries, was a key feature.

• ***Temptation Island*** – four attractive couples were put on an island resort, and their 'coupledom' shown. Then one or other of the couple were required to interact with and go on dates with attractive singles (not their partner), while being plied with alcohol. The most salacious moments of the resultant flirting were then shown to the other partner in the couple, to see how they would react.

• ***Survivor*** – another reality/game show, now in its eighth variation, because of huge popularity. Two teams or 'tribes' were taken to a remote location, and forced to 'survive' by their skills, wits and relationships. A series of challenges was imposed on them, to see who would cope and who wouldn't. Individuals were steadily voted off the show (by players, not the audience), until only two remained. The 'jury' (made up of evicted players) then chose a winner, who received $1,000,000. Product placement, as for example the reward of Mountain Dew lemonade at the end of a challenge, was a key feature. (Curious footnote: The game was invented by Sir Bob Geldoff.)

• ***Australian Idol*** – stage managed by a record company, this show involved a series of auditions of entertainment hopefuls, who were shown going through their paces. Of the original several dozen, 12 were picked by audience participation, and then these gradually wittled down to one winner, who was then given a recording contract.

• ***Popstars*** – a variation on the above, but without audience participation, in which a group of wannabes were gradually trained how to act like pop singers.

• *The Bachelor* – one guy and 20 girls; he had to choose one as his partner. The girls all competed furiously for the one man, and of course the prize and glory.

• *The Bachelorette* – one girl and 20 guys – the same idea as *The Bachelor*, only with the genders reversed.

Voyeurism, image and media manipulation in other texts

The idea of media manipulation is not a new one. Here is a small selection of significant film texts with something to say about the subject.

Films about voyerism

• *Rear Window* (1954) – an all time classic thriller by Alfred Hitchcock, in which a man confined to a wheelchair (James Stewart) takes to watching his neighbours through the window of his apartment, and accidentally sees a murder. With the help of his girlfriend (Grace Kelly), he must do something about it before the murderer finds out he has been observed and takes action.

• *Psycho* (1961) – another Hitchcock masterpiece, in which a madman (Anthony Perkins) spies on a beautiful young woman (Janet Leigh) before killing her in the shower.

• *Sex, lies and videotape* (1989) – the award winning debut film of Steven Soderberg, about a young man (James Spader) who videotapes people's intimate confessions about their sex lives, in the process unravelling all sorts of emotional issues.

• *One Hour Photo* (2002) – starring Robin Williams as Seymour, the shy photo development clerk who becomes obsessed with a family whose shots he develops and starts spying on them, with unexpected consequences.

Films about image

• *Pretty Woman* (1990) – directed by Garry Marshall, starring Julia Roberts and Richard Gere: a pretty 'hooker' is picked up by a wealthy businessman, and becomes his consort; then he falls in love with her. This Cinderella story is all about the transformation of the tacky hooker into a glamorous 'lady'.

• *Strictly Ballroom* (1992) – directed by Baz Luhrmann – about an 'ugly duckling' woman who is gradually transformed into a glamorous star.

• *Pret-a-Porter* (1994) – directed by Robert Altman – an expose of the image-obsessed fashion industry.

• *Citizen Kane*, written and directed by Orson Welles (1941) – an all time cult favourite, about a media mogul (Charles Foster Kane), based loosely on the real life newspaper tycoon William Randolf Hearst, who amasses a fortune by controlling the news, but who loses his soul in the process.

• *Network* directed by Sidney Lumet (1976) – a black satire about a newsreader (Peter Finch) who is sacked because of falling ratings, and in desperation announces his intention of committing suicide live on air. This confronts the network with the ethical dilemma – will they let him do it to ensure huge ratings, or will they stop him for humanitarian reasons?

• *Broadcast News* directed by James Brooks (1987) – an insider's look at current affairs television, with a triangle involving the handsome but slow-witted anchorman (William Hurt), who pretends to know everything, and the real brains behind the show, his producer (Holly Hunter).

• *Wag the Dog* directed by Barry Levinson (1997) – a disturbing parable about political construction of current affairs. When the US president is about to get caught in a sex scandal just before an election, one of his advisors hires a Hollywood producer (Dustin Hoffman) to fake a small foreign war which the President can heroically end. A clever black comedy about the way 'reality' can be constructed by politicians in cahoots with the media.

• *EdTV* directed by Ron Howard (1998) – by the strangest of coincidences, this rather less stylised and more plausible take on 'reality TV' came out in exactly the same year as The Truman Show. It has an everyman character (Matthew McConaughey) put on TV 24 hours a day for the viewing pleasure of the audience. Unlike Truman, Ed knows he is being filmed – as all 'reality TV' 'stars' do – and the movie charts his progress from cheerful acceptance of the experience to rebellion and horror, when he realises that he is trapped in the non-stop media circus as long as the channel wishes. Finally the only way he can stop the show is by threatening to expose the TV chairman, at which point the exploitation suddenly stops, to everyone's great relief.

Other popular (film) texts about the questionable (and often dangerously subjective) nature of 'reality' include

• *Total Recall* (1990) – directed by Paul Verhoeven, and based on a Philip Dick (*Blade Runner*) story, it concerns Douglas (Arnold

Schwarzenegger), who wants to go on a 'virtual holiday' to Mars, by means of memory implants. The implants go horribly wrong and he ends up not sure who he is in reality.

• *Groundhog Day* (1995) – directed by Harold Ramis, it concerns a TV reporter (Bill Murray) and his producer (Andie McDowell) sent to cover a small town event involving a 'groundhog' (rodent) festival, who discovers that he is locked into repeating the same day over and over again. No matter what he does to alter the reality of the day, he always wakes up to the same day.

• *Pleasantville* (1998) – directed by Gary Ross, concerns a lonely boy, David (Toby McGuire) who has become obsessed with a 1950s black and white sitcom (of that name) about a perfect small American town, and wishes he could live in the world of the show. His wish is granted, and he and his sister (Reese Witherspoon) find themselves in the black and white world of the show. Soon however they start rebelling against the stifling conformity of the show. (A very interesting point of contrast to *The Truman Show*, which also comments on an idealised American town and its idealised inhabitants.)

• *The Matrix* (1999) – directed by the Wachowski brothers, this posits the idea that 'reality' as we know it is a fiction constructed by a vast supercomputer. However ace hacker Neo (Keanu Reeves) discovers the plot, and together with Morpheus (Laurence Fishburn) and Trinity (Carrie-Ann Fisher) sets out to rebel against the machines who have taken over the world. Also two sequels.

• *Vanilla Sky* (2001) – directed by Cameron Crowe: a rich playboy, David (Tom Cruise), is careless of his relationship with an old girlfriend (Cameron Diaz) and has dumped her for a new one (Penelope Cruz). However, the old girlfriend gets her revenge by causing a near fatal car crash. David wakes up to find he is a totally different person, and perhaps all that he takes for real is in fact a dream.

The number of print texts on this topic which are readily available is limited. Here however is a short selection of recommended readings which can be easily accessed:

Print texts on the genre

• *Brave New World*, by Aldous Huxley (1932) – about a future world so tightly controlled (by world 'controllers') that no hint of human history is allowed to be known by the general public. The citizens are totally brainwashed from birth, via hypnopaedia and community ceremonies which indoctrinate them. Huxley also made his comment on the media with the idea of 'feelies' – tasteless synthetic sensory movies which allow viewers to feel and smell the actors. This is considered a major classic, and one of the key literary reference points on the theme.

• *The Wife of Martin Guerre,* by Janet Lewis (1941) – a modern classic about a medieval wife (Bertrande Guerre) whose husband goes to war, never to return; years later a stranger who looks exactly like Martin offers himself as the husband, and she has to resist the temptation of accepting the false 'Martin' for the real one.

• *Nineteen Eighty-Four*, by George Orwell (1947) – the other classic text about a nightmare state where everything citizens do is monitored by the all-powerful Party, and its dictator head 'Big Brother' (a sort of Stalin figure). The Party controls all information, rewriting history and current affairs at will to suit current political needs. The image of Big Brother is everywhere. And all citizens are constantly under surveillance by TV screens which play non-stop patriotic material, and also conceal hidden cameras. This alone links the text to *The Truman Show*. It is the text most closely associated with the term 'brainwashing'. As well as the term 'Big Brother' (for an intrusive authoritarian state), Orwell coined the terms 'thought police' and 'doublethink' (for believing the opposite of what is valid for political reasons).

• *To Kill a Mockingbird*, by Harper Lee (1961) – the great Civil Rights novel about a small town girl who grows up in her understanding of how we judge others; Scout and her brother are obsessed as children with the neighbourhood 'monster', Boo, only to find out that he is a shy, disabled individual; the town is obsessed with black man Tom Robinson, seeing him as bad because he is black, when the truth is that he is good, and the white people who accuse him are the bad ones.

• **'The Edge'**, by Sylvia Plath (1963) – a searing poem by the great feminist poet, who died young, about the way image controls a woman.

• *The Female Eunuch*, by Germaine Greer (1970) – in which the celebrated Australian feminist argued that women are kept subjugated by the 'patriarchy', and made to conform to male-dictated models of appearance and behaviour.

• *Ways of Seeing*, by John Berger (1978) – the British art critic and cultural historian's landmark work on the way we observe; made a huge impact with its assertion that men look at women, and women have been historically indoctrinated with the idea that they are objects to be consumed by the male gaze.

• *The Beauty Myth*, by Naomi Wolf (1992) – in which the American feminist argues that patriarchal society has engaged in a 'backlash' against women's liberation, by attacking women's sense of themselves as represented by their appearance: 'The more legal and material hindrances women have broken through, the more strictly and heavily and cruelly images of female beauty have come to weigh upon us...During the past decade, women breached the power structure; meanwhile, eating disorders rose exponentially and cosmetic surgery became the fastest-growing specialty...pornography became the main media category, ahead of legitimate films and records combined, and thirty-three thousand American women told researchers that they would rather lose ten to fifteen pounds than achieve any other goal...More women have more money and power...than we have ever had before; but in terms of how we feel about ourselves physically, we may actually be worse off than our unliberated grandmothers.'

Sample Exam Response

'Images shape our lives, for good or ill.'

Discuss this statement with reference to your prescribed text and related texts of your own choosing.

General introduction to the topic with examples

We live in a media saturated world, surrounded by images. Billboards show us attractive young models emerging out of chocolate bars, or the eyes of *Big Brother* (the TV show). Movie posters feature Keanu Reeves in dark glasses in character for *The Matrix*, or dramatic shots from popular movies. Magazines confront us with Kylie Minogue's famous bottom, or Nicole Kidman's latest success. Turn on the TV, and we have programs which offer us their representations of 'reality' – whether it be news, current affairs, game shows or those oddly named confections, 'reality TV' shows. Sometimes, the real and the image is completely confused, as in the famous example of Arnold Schwarzenegger becoming Governor of California because he was a movie star – a startling example of synthesising the *image* of an action man hero with the real role of a politician. There is no doubt that the media, and the images they pour into our lives, have a huge influence on us. Whether it is a good influence or not is wide open to debate.

Detailed discussion of the pre-scribed text

Certainly, Peter Weir's film *The Truman Show* offers us a decidedly critical look at media manipulation. The title character is seen by all the world. Images of Truman in the bathroom, in the car, at the office, gardening, talking to his buddy Marlon – are everywhere. But – and this is the catch – he doesn't even know it. He is a product, and no one has let him in on the secret. His wife Meryl, the perfect 50s style housewife, is blond, blue eyed, dimpled – a picture postcard wife. His home town, Seahaven, is as perfect as Disneyland – and just as false. In this biting satire of TV, God is a director. Behind the mockery of a life that Truman lives is the all-powerful Cristof – the man in the moon – who fine tunes every moment in Truman's life, every bit of product placement, every sly promotion of a domestic appliance. He has crafted the whole show as an entertainment and a commercial – that's the genius of the show – and Truman doesn't even know.

How the text shapes meaning

Yet the mockery doesn't just stop at exposing image manipulation – the glitzy sets, the huge cast of extras, the crane shots, the synthetic dialogue (piped from Cristof to the actors playing Truman's relatives and friends). It moves a stage further. When Truman finds out that his whole life is a fraud, he rebels. He rejects his picture-perfect but fake wife, and goes after the girl he loves. He escapes from Seahaven, braving everything Cristof can throw at him, and finds the wall which is the end of the vast set. And he goes through the door in the wall into real life. Thus Weir and Niccol (the scriptwriter) signal their underlying message: that we (the viewers) need to resist the power of the media, and find our own individuality. We need to challenge the images that seduce and bind us, and make our own decisions. Because *The Truman Show* is as much about our own enchantment with images – of celebrities, of glamorous lifestyle, of escapist dreams – as it is about the imaginary Truman. Images *do* shape us, but perhaps we need to regard them a little more sceptically than we do.

Just such a rejection of the popular culture is to be found at the heart of another text, though one vastly different to *The Truman Show*. *To Kill a Mockingbird* doesn't once mention the mass

*Related text –
contrast of
text type but
similar
themes*
media, because the novel is set in the 1930s and the media have nothing to do with the way people think. Harper Lee's book is however an exposé of another type of image distortion – not the false imagery of the media but the false imagery of racism. Lee prepares readers for her theme with a simple, indeed childlike example. The two kids who are the main characters, Scout and her brother Jem, are convinced that Boo Radley, a recluse who lives in a derelict house just down the road, is a monster who comes out at night and slakes his mad appetite with blood. The truth of course is that he is just a poor intellectually disabled person who means no harm. It takes till the end of the novel for Scout and Jem to discover this, but it is a vital lesson. More mainstream, and more significant perhaps, is the novel's other lesson about image. Tom Robinson has been jailed for alleged rape of a white girl, Mayella Ewell. Because he is black, and this is the Deep South, an all white jury finds him guilty, though he is obviously innocent. In coming to terms with this shocking idea, Scout and Jem realise that people think in prejudiced ways, and that the image they have of others (particularly black people) is vastly different from the reality. Like Truman, they rebel against this falsity, though the author is honest enough to suggest that their resistance will make no difference to a racist time and place.

*Related text
in different
medium*
All around us are images. Look at TV ads. They present images of domestic perfection – the perfect Mum, the perfect home, the perfect meal, the perfect car. But are we being conned? Consider the ad – by a major hamburger fast food chain – about the latest salad offering. A cute, freckly little boy looks straight into the camera and talks about how much he loves this new salad, because it pleases his Mum, because it's healthy. His Mum is shown, smiling happily. Then we cut to the salad. It looks delicious, *and* healthy. Then there's the tagline about how good for you the product is. The images – of child, mother and salad – sell the product. We look and we believe. Or do we? Millions probably will. Images as cunningly crafted as this one are hard to resist.

*Conclusion
return to topic*
For good or ill? Probably both. There's nothing wrong with a little escapism, or fantasy, and who doesn't like looking at gorgeous people, or clothes, or houses? But when the images are meant deliberately to manipulate us, as with the ad – or even lie to us – maybe we should be concerned. One thing's for sure – knowing how images are shaped, and catching the manipulators in the act, makes us that much harder to con. And that's got to be good.

Titles in this series so far

The Accidental Tourist
Angela's Ashes
Antigone
Away
The Bell Jar
The Blooding
Brave New World / Blade Runner
Breaker Morant
Briar Rose
Brilliant Lies
The Brush-Off
Cabaret
Cat's Eye
The Chant of Jimmie Blacksmith
Cloudstreet
The Collector
Cosi
The Crucible
The Divine Wind
Diving for Pearls
Educating Rita
Elli
Emma & Clueless
Falling
Fly Away Peter
Follow Your Heart
The Freedom of the City
Frontline
Gattaca
Girl with a Pearl Earring
Going Home
A Good Scent from a Strange Mountain
Great Expectations
The Great Gatsby
Hamlet
The Handmaid's Tale
Hard Times
Henry Lawson's Stories
Highways to a War
I for Isobel
An Imaginary Life
In Between
In Country
In the Lake of the Woods
The Inheritors
The Journey Area of Study
King Lear
The Kitchen God's Wife
A Lesson before Dying

Letters from the Inside
The Life and Crimes of Harry Lavender
Lives of Girls and Women
Lionheart
The Longest Memory
Looking for Alibrandi
The Lost Salt Gift of Blood
Macbeth
Maestro
A Man for All Seasons
Medea
Montana 1948
My Brother Jack
My Left Foot
My Name is Asher Lev
My Place
Night
Nineteen Eighty-Four
No Great Mischief
Oedipus Rex
Of Love and Shadows
One True Thing
Only the Heart
Othello
The Outsider
Paper Nautilus
The Player
Pride and Prejudice
Rabbit-Proof Fence
Raw
Remembering Babylon
The Riders
Schindler's List
Scission
Shakespeare in Love
The Shipping News
Sometimes Gladness
Stolen
Strictly Ballroom
Summer of the Seventeenth Doll
Things Fall Apart
Tirra Lirra by the River
Travels with my Aunt
The Truman Show
We All Fall Down
What's Eating Gilbert Grape
The Wife of Martin Guerre
Wild Cat Falling
Witness
Women of the Sun
Wrack